EAR

# The Fifth Elephant

**Terry Pratchett's**

**The Fifth Elephant**

*adapted by*

**Stephen Briggs**

**Methuen Drama**

Novel copyright © 1999 Terry Pratchett
Adaptation copyright © 2002 Stephen Briggs

The authors have asserted their moral rights

Methuen Publishing Limited Reg. No. 3543167

A CIP catalogue record for this book is available
from the British Library

ISBN 0 413 77115 6

Typeset by SX Composing DTP, Rayleigh, Essex
Printed and bound in Great Britain by Cox & Wyman Ltd

# Introduction

## All the Discworld's a Stage

The first people *ever* to dramatise the Discworld, in any form, were the Studio Theatre Club in Abingdon, Oxon. That was in 1991, with *Wyrd Sisters*.

We had already staged our own adaptations of other works: Monty Python's *Life of Brian* and *Holy Grail* – and Tom Sharpe's *Porterhouse Blue* and *Blott on the Landscape*. We were looking for something new when someone said, 'Try Terry Pratchett – you'll like him.' So I ventured into the previously uncharted territory of the 'Fantasy' section of the local bookstore ('Here be dragons'). I read a Terry Pratchett book; I liked it. I read all of them. I wrote to Terry and asked if we could stage *Wyrd Sisters* . He said 'Yes'.

*Wyrd Sisters* sold out.

So did *Mort* the year after.

So did *Guards! Guards!*, *Men at Arms*, *Maskerade*, *Jingo* and *Carpe Jugulum* in the years after that. In fact, 'sold out' is too modest an expression. 'Oversold very quickly so that by the time the local newspaper mentioned it was on we'd had to close the booking office' is nearer the mark.

My casts were all happy enough to read whichever book we were staging, and to read others in the canon, too. The books stand on their own, but some knowledge of the wider Discworld ethos is essential when adapting the stories, and can also help directors to find out where it's all coming from, and the actors with their characterisations.

The Discworld novels have been getting longer (and darker) as the years pass and it is a problem trying to put over the plot while still meeting the over-riding target for amdram – getting into the pub before closing. The important thing was to decide what the basic plot was: anything which didn't contribute to that was liable to be dropped in order to keep the play flowing. Favourite scenes, even favourite characters, have on occasions had to be dumped. These are hard decisions but the book has to work as a *play*. You can't get four hundred pages of novel into two and a half hours on stage without sacrifices.

Each play also offers a challenge to directors in working out who can double for whom when working with a smaller cast. You'll see from the cast list, which follows this introduction, how *we* covered all the roles.

Although the majority of our audiences are 'fans', I've tried to remember when writing the plays that not *all* the audience will be steeped in Discworld lore. Some of them may just be normal theatre-goers who've never read a fantasy novel in their whole lives; humorous fantasy may not be their 'thing', but I wouldn't want them to feel they were watching something which had been typed on an Enigma machine.

The books are episodic and have a sort of 'cinematic' construction; this can be a difficult concept to incorporate into a play. Set changes slow down the action. Any scene change that takes more than twenty to thirty seconds means you've lost the audience. Even *ten*-second changes, if repeated often enough, will lead to loss of interest. I've been to see many productions of the plays and the best have been those that have used bare stages or composite sets – leaving the majority of the 'scene-changing' to the lighting technician. The golden rule is: if you *can* do it without scene-shifting, *do* it without scene-shifting. It's a concept that has served radio drama very well (everyone *knows* that radio has the best scenery). And Shakespeare managed very well without it, too.

The plays do, however, call for some unusual props. Over the years, many of these have been made by my casts and crew: large hourglasses for Death's house, shadow puppets, archaic rifles, dragon-scorched books and, of course, Detritus's massive portable siege crossbow for *The Fifth Elephant*. Other, more specialised props were put 'out to contract': Death's sword and scythe, an orangutan, Detritus's head and hands, a Death of Rats, a Greebo, Scraps the dog and two swamp dragons (one an elaborate hand puppet and one with a fire-proof compartment in its bottom for a flight scene).

Since the Studio Theatre Club started the trend in 1991, Terry and I have had many enquiries about staging the books – from as far afield as Finland, South Africa, Indonesia, Australia, Bermuda and the Czech Republic (as well as

Sheffield, Aberdeen, Exeter and the Isle of Man). Royalties from the five plays administered by *me* have raised over £35,000 so far for the Orangutan Foundation.

So how did our productions actually go? We enjoyed them. Our audiences seemed to enjoy them (after all, some of them were prepared, year after year, to travel down to Abingdon in Oxfordshire from Taunton, Newcastle-upon-Tyne, Ipswich, Basingstoke and . . . well, Oxford). Terry seems to enjoy them, too. He says that many of our members look as though they have been recruited straight off the streets of Ankh-Morpork. He says that several of them were born to play the 'rude mechanicals' in Vitoller's troupe in *Wyrd Sisters*, and that in his mind's eye the famous Ankh-Morpork City Watch *are* the players of the Studio Theatre Club.

I'm sure these were meant to be compliments.

## The Fifth Elephant
By the time we staged *The Fifth Elephant* in 1999, we knew that the Discworld plays were a winner . . . though we'd learned that the flourishing trade in other groups staging the plays meant that we couldn't afford to take full houses for granted. They're still full, but we do have to work a bit now to achieve that.

As with all the adaptations, there were difficult choices about which scenes should be sacrificed to try and keep the play down to a reasonable running time. We had also realised that Abingdon's medieval Unicorn Theatre was a part of the package; it has its shortcomings, but its ambience of cobwebby oak beams and thick stone walls contributed much to the original success of the shows.

This dramatisation was written with the Unicorn Theatre's restrictions, and the number of players I expected to have available, in mind. Really complicated scenic effects were virtually impossible. Basically, we had a bare stage with an on-stage balcony at the back with a small curtained area beneath it. Anyone thinking of staging a Discworld play can be as imaginative as they like – call upon the might of Industrial Light & Magic, if it's within their budget. But *The Fifth Elephant can* be staged with only a relatively modest outlay on special effects and the notes that accompany the text are intended to be a guide for those, like us, with limited budgets. Bigger groups, with teams of experts on hand, can let their imaginations run wild!

In short, though, our experience and that of other groups is that it pays to work hard on getting the costumes and lighting right, and to keep the scenery to little more than, perhaps, a few changes of level on a composite set. There's room for all sorts of ideas here. The Discworld, as it says in the books, is your mollusc.

Characterisation: Within the constraints of what is known and vital about each character, there is still room for flexibility of interpretation. With the main roles, though, you have to recognise that your audiences will expect them to look as much like the book descriptions as possible. Most drama clubs don't have a vast range from which to choose, though, and it's the acting that's more important than the look of the player when it comes down to it! *The Discworld Companion* gives some background information about the City Watch, Lord Vetinari and Lady Sybil, though keen performers may want to try to read all 'their' character's books.

Costumes: We played most of the Ankh-Morpork characters in a form of Victorian dress, with the Überwald citizens and guards having a turn-of-the-century Russian look about them. The dwarfs were in leather armour, boots, helmets, etc. and we put our human werewolves (Wolfgang and his crew) into suitably adapted SS uniforms (hired from Angel's & Berman's) – this gives them the right look of threatening, psychopathic evil before Wolfgang even speaks his first line.

Scenery: Virtually none. Our major set-piece was a white backcloth (well, *floor*cloth, really) which was quickly set and struck for the outdoor snow scenes. Surprisingly effective (despite my cast's initial cynicism!). Apart from that, there were just the odd bits of furniture.

Special Effects: Other little bits and pieces, not covered in the text, included: *dog and wolf-heads*. We had our Gaspode all in black, but with a scruffy mongrel's head incorporated into a baseball cap. Gavin and our werewolves, when wolves, also wore black, but with proprietory wolf masks. Angua and Wolfgang wore prominent pendants (Wolfie, a pentagram, Angua, her Watch badge), duplicates of which were also sported by their werewolf doubles, so the audience could tell who was who.

Oh, and a word on pronunciation . . . Having seen many of the plays staged, pronunciation of the names seems sometimes to be a stumbling block. Here are some pointers:

| | |
|---|---|
| Ankh-Morpork | Ankh, as in 'bank', Morpork as in 'more pork', with the stress in the city's name on the second syllable – Ankh-*Mor*pork. |
| Vetinari | Long 'a' and stress the third syllable – Vetin*ah*-ri. |
| Angua | Hard 'g'. Preferred pronunciation is *An*-gew-ah, though *An*-gwa is also acceptable. |
| Wolfgang | Wolf like 'wolf' for Morporkians, but like 'volf' (short 'o') for those from überwald. |
| Inigo | Short 'i's – *In*-i-go |
| Igor | *Ee*gor. *Not* Eyegor! |
| Detritus | Duh-*try*-tuss |
| Scone | Everyone except Vimes pronounces it with a long 'o'. Vimes, man of the people, pronounces it 'Scon' throughout. |

Thinking of staging it? Although Methuen control the amateur rights for *The Fifth Elephant*, Terry and I are keen to know which of our plays are being staged where, so do feel free to write to me or email me with your production dates, just in case one of us can get to see your show. I also have some stocks of a snazzy überwald League of Temperance badge . . . I can be contacted either via Methuen, or via email at sbriggs@cix.co.uk

Stephen Briggs
February 2002

# The Fifth Elephant

*The Fifth Elephant*, dramatised by Stephen Briggs, was first presented by the Studio Theatre Club at the Unicorn Theatre, Abingdon, on Tuesday 23 November 1999. The cast was as follows:

| | |
|---|---|
| **Gaspode** | Nigel Tait |
| **Lord Vetinari/Wolfgang** | Stephen Briggs |
| **Cdr Vimes** | Trev Collins |
| **Lady Sybil** | Sharon Stone |
| **Capt Carrot** | Mark Cowper |
| **Cpl Littlebottom/Glum Sister** | Karen Hale |
| **Sgt Detritus** | John Kirchhoff |
| **Willikins/Sgt Colonescue** | Keith Franklin |
| **Inigo Skimmer** | Mike Davey |
| **Sgt Angua** | Kath Leighton |
| **Rhys Rhysson** | Graham Cook |
| **Albrecht Albrechtson/Glum Sister** | Jenny Bonnin |
| **Dee/Glum Sister** | Claire Aston |
| **Lady Margolotta** | Val Shelley |
| **Igor** | Peter Laurence |
| **Baroness** | Victoria Martin |
| **Baron** | Dave Weaver |
| **Chief Bandit** | Tim Arnot |
| **Dwarf Guard** | Robin Allen |
| **Gavin** | Paul Burton |
| **Other Bandits, Werewolves, etc.** | Simon Read, Pam Aird, Giles Martin, Ian Weeden |

*Director* Stephen Briggs
*Lighting/Effects* Colin James
*Sound* Phil Evans
*Stage Manager* Dave Weaver

*The Fifth Elephant* was subsequently presented by HMS Collingwood at the Millennium Hall, HMS Collingwood on Tuesday 20 March 2001.

| | |
|---|---|
| **Gaspode** | Nicola Cooper |
| **Lord Vetinari/Igor** | Phil Pennington |
| **Cdr. Vimes** | Peter Trott |
| **Lady Sybil** | Becky James |
| **Capt. Carrot** | Paul Lewis |
| **Sgt. Littlebottom** | Liz Sutton |
| **Sgt. Detritus** | Matt Blackhurst |
| **Sgt. Colonescue** | David Barlow |
| **Inigo Skimmer** | Mark Rutley |
| **Sgt. Angua** | Jane Blatch |
| **Rhys Rhysson** | Alisa Govern |
| **Albrecht Albrechtson** | Virginia Hodge |
| **Dee/Glum Sister** | Karen Headley |
| **Lady Margolotta** | Sally Dixon |
| **Wolfgang** | Jason Saunders |
| **Baroness** | Clare Evans |
| **Baron** | Chris Gainey |
| **Chief Bandit/Glum Sister** | Angie Blackhurst |
| **Gavin/Willikins** | Chris Blackhurst |
| **The Other Two Glum Sisters** | Fleur, Katrina Trott |
| **Other Bandits, Werewolves, etc.** | Emma Luffingham, Matt Law, Michael Gainey, Samantha King, Katie Blackhurst, Adam Gainey, Max Barletta |

*Director* Chris Gainey
*Lighting/Effects* Gareth Trott
*Sound* Keith Masson
*Stage Manager* Bob Bell

# Act One

## Scene One

*Bare stage. Gaspode is discovered, on. He 'sees' the audience.*

**Gaspode**   Er . . . 'Woof, woof' . Wotcha. Gaspode's the name. Yes. I'm a dog and yes, I *can* talk. Well spotted. Bit of a magical accident a few years back. You know how it is on Discworld . . . 's'appenin' all the time . . . It's a dog's life, you know, bein' a dog. Thrown into the river with a brick in a sack, I was, when I was a pup. Lucky for me, it was the Ankh, most polluted river in the multiverse, so I was able to *walk* ashore inside the sack . . . When you're a dog, see, you face the eternal dichotomy. The essential schizophrenia wossname. See, we all want nothing more than to have a master and warm place in front of the fire of life. On the other hand, we all 'ave the wolf within . . . we rebel against any restriction on our freedom to roam, and to roll in whatever we like . . . Most dogs, o'course, aren't aware of all this. *My* problem is, I am.

**Lord Vetinari** *enters.*

Oh, 'ere we are . . . play's startin'. This is the ruler of Ankh-Morpork, Lord V . . ., er, Lord Ve . . ., Lord *Vetinari*. Sorry – it's a dog thing. We 'ave real problems with the, er, *v-e-t* word. Also the *b-a-t-h* word, y'know. And the *b-a-d-d-o-g* thing? Generations of livin' with people has played merry hell with canine self-confidence.

**Lord Vetinari** *casts* **Gaspode** *a glance.*

Woof . . . ?

**Gaspode** *exits. A moment, as* **Lord Vetinari** *stands, waiting for* **Vimes** *to arrive.* **Vimes** *and* **Carrot** *rush on, out of breath.*

**Vimes**   Sorry we're late, sir.

**Lord Vetinari**   Oh, *are* you late, Commander? I really hadn't noticed. What do you know about the Fifth Elephant, Commander?

**Vimes** (*confidently*)   I know there's a dwarfish legend that the Disc used to be supported by five elephants instead of the four we got now, sir.

**Carrot**   Did you know that dwarf scientists believe that the elephants, being such huge beasts, have bones of living rock and iron and nerves of gold for better conductivity over the vast distances involved? My people believe that the fifth elephant lost its footing and fell off the turtle shell and drifted into a curved orbit before eventually crashing down in the area now occupied by the Ramtop Mountains.

**Vimes**   Thank you, Captain, I *did* know that. Anyway, my lord, after the big crash, tons of rock thrown up by the impact fell back, covering and compressing the corpse, and the rest, after millennia of underground cooking and rendering, is history. The Ramtops' plentiful underground deposits of gold, iron and fat are believed to be due to this legendary catastrophe. Sir.

**Lord Vetinari**   Well done, Commander. And what about Bonk? (**Vetinari** *pronounces it here as written.*)

**Vimes**   Sir . . . ?

**Carrot**   The river or the town, my lord?

**Lord Vetinari**   Ah, Captain, you have long ago ceased to surprise me. I was referring to the town.

**Carrot**   One of the major towns in überwald, my lord. Exports – precious metals, leather, timber and of course fat from the Schmaltzberg fat mines . . .

**Vimes**   There's a *place* called Bonk?

**Carrot**   Yes, sir. But in *their* language '*Morpork*' sounds like an item of ladies' underwear.

**Vimes**   Does it? Which item, exactly . . . ?

**Lord Vetinari** (*interrupting*)   Something extremely important will be happening there in a few weeks. Something that will be vital to the future prosperity of Ankh-Morpork.

**Carrot**   The crowning of the Low King, my lord?

**Vimes**   Is there some kind of circular that goes around to everyone apart from me?

**Carrot**   The dwarf community has been talking about little else for months, sir.

**Vimes**   Aah. You mean all the riots? The fights every night in the dwarf bars?

**Lord Vetinari**   Captain Carrot is correct, Vimes. It will be a grand occasion, attended by the representatives of many governments and from Überwald's many principalities. As you know, the Low King only rules those areas of Überwald that are below ground.

**Vimes** (*with careful irony*)   Oh, of course, sir.

**Lord Vetinari**   Borogravia and Genua will be there. Probably even Klatch.

**Vimes**   Klatch? But they're even further away than we are. Why would they bother going? Hold on – where's the money?

**Lord Vetinari**   Commander?

**Vimes**   There's got to be money behind this.

**Lord Vetinari**   A large country, überwald. Dark, mysterious, ancient.

**Carrot**   Huge untapped reserves of coal and iron ore. And fat, of course.

**Vimes**   Fat? But we make our own don't we? All those renderers near the slaugherhouse district.

**Carrot**   Not such good quality, sir. And Ankh-Morpork uses a great many candles. There are so many uses for fats and tallow, sir. We couldn't possibly supply ourselves.

**Vimes**   Ah. Trade. Got it.

**Lord Vetinari**   Obviously I hope to improve our trading links with the various nations within Überwald. The situation there is volatile in the extreme. Do you *know* much about Überwald, Commander?

**Vimes**   Only that it's not really a country . . .

**Carrot**   It's more what you get *before* you get countries. It's mainly fortified towns and little principalities with no real borders and lots of forest in between. There's always feuding. No real laws and lots of banditry . . .

**Vimes** (*not quite under his breath*)   So unlike the home life of our own dear city.

**Lord Vetinari** *gives him an impassive glance.*

**Carrot**   . . . in Überwald, the dwarfs and trolls *still* don't get on. There are large areas controlled by feudal vampire or werewolf clans. It is to be hoped that things will improve, however, and Überwald will, happily, be joining the community of nations.

**Lord Vetinari** *and* **Vimes** *exchange a look.*

**Lord Vetinari**   Well put. But until that joysome day, Überwald remains a mystery inside a riddle wrapped in an enigma.

**Vimes**   Let me see if I've got it right. Überwald is like this big suet pudding that everyone's suddenly noticed and now with this coronation as an excuse we've all got to rush there with knife, fork and spoon to shovel as much on our plates as possible?

**Lord Vetinari** (*after a brief pause*)   Your grasp of political reality is masterly, Vimes. Ankh-Morpork must send a representative. An ambassador, as it were.

**Vimes**   You're not suggesting *I* should go.

**Lord Vetinari**   I couldn't possibly send the Commander of the City Watch.

**Vimes** *relaxes*.

I shall send the Duke of Ankh-Morpork instead.

**Vimes** *tenses again*.

**Carrot**   But that's you, too, sir.

**Vimes**   Thank you, Carrot, I *do* know that!

**Lord Vetinari**   They set a lot of store by rank . . .

**Vimes**   I'm not being ordered to go to Überwald!

**Lord Vetinari**   Ordered, your grace? Good heavens, I must have misunderstood Lady Sybil . . .. She told me yesterday that a holiday a long way from Ankh-Morpork would do you the world of good . . .

**Vimes**   Sybil . . . ?

**Lord Vetinari**   Oh dear, I do hope I haven't caused some marital misunderstanding . . .

**Vimes**   But I can't leave the city now . . . there's so much to do! You *know* I'm no good at diplomatic talk.

**Lord Vetinari**   On the contrary, Vimes. You have amazed the diplomatic corps here in Ankh-Morpork. They're not used to plain speech, it confuses them. That can be quite effective.

**Vimes** (*a little desperately*)   But you don't want me saying stuff like: 'How 'bout selling us some of your fat really cheap', do you?

**Lord Vetinari**   You will not be required to do *any* negotiating, Commander. That will be dealt with by one of my clerks, who will set up the temporary Embassy. *You* will simply be as ducal as you can. You'll need a retinue, of course. I would suggest Sergeant Angua, Sergeant Detritus and Corporal Littlebottom.

**Carrot**   Ah yes, my lord. A werewolf, a troll and a dwarf. Ethnic minorities, sir.

**Lord Vetinari**   But in Überwald, they are ethnic *majorities*. They all herald from Überwald I believe. Their presence will speak volumes.

**Vimes**   Sorry?

**Carrot**   It will show them that Ankh-Morpork is a multi-cultural society, sir.

**Lord Vetinari**   Good. I will have a semaphore message sent to Überwald immediately.

*He passes* **Vimes** *the invitation and briefing notes.*

Here. You will be more fully briefed later. Do give my regards to the duchess. I'm sure you can find your own way out.

**Lord Vetinari** *departs.*

**Vimes**   He always does that. He knows I hate being married to a duchess.

**Carrot**   But I thought you and Lady Sybil . . .

**Vimes**   Oh, being married to Sybil is fine. It's just the Duchess bit I can't take. Get Angua, Detritus and Littlebottom to report to me first thing tomorrow.

**Carrot**   Yessir.

**Vimes** (*he looks at the invitation*)   I've never heard of the Low King of the Dwarfs. I thought that 'king' in dwarfish just meant a sort of senior engineer.

**Carrot**   Ah well. The Low King is rather special. It all starts with the Scone of Stone, sir.

**Vimes**   The what?

**Carrot**    Perhaps we could make a little detour on the way back to the Yard, sir. To the Dwarf Bread Museum. It could make things clearer.

**Scene Two**

*The street outside the Dwarf Bread Museum. On-stage, as yet unlit, is an empty podium with* **Detritus** *on guard beside it.* **Gaspode** *enters.*

**Gaspode**    Wotcha. Now then, the Low King and the Scone of Stone . . . Werl, the Scone of Stone is pretty much what it sounds like. Dwarf bread is both a delicacy and a battle weapon. It contains all you need to sustain you for days, mainly by causing you to perform miracles of endurance in order to get somewhere where you don't have to eat dwarf bread. Dwarf cake is similar, but thicker. A properly thrown slice of dwarf bread is a fearsome weapon, especially in view of its boomerang properties. It's legendary for its hardness and its inedible qualities. The Scone of Stone is, well, to all intents and purposes it's a lump of rock with fossilised currants in it. It is also an important relic of dwarf lore on which the Low King is crowned and a replica is kept in the Dwarf Bread Museum in Ankh-Morpork. Now, the Low King. The Low King is the final court of appeal for everything relating to dwarf law – safety below ground, marriage, inheritance, rules for dealing with disputes. He has advisers, but he has the last word. The Low King is . . . well, elected, really. By a lot of senior dwarfs, after having taken soundings about public opinion. He is *crowned* on the Scone of Stone and he sits on it to give his judgements because all the Low Kings have done it for over fifteen hundred years. It's *tradition*.

**Vimes** *and* **Carrot** *enter.*

**Vimes**    . . . Oh, I get it. You always do something because it's always been done.

**Carrot**   Things are a bit different this year, sir. Tempers are a bit stretched. The whole process has been called into question by the dwarfs of the biggest dwarf city outside Überwald.

**Vimes** (*not quite believing it*)   Ankh-Morpork?

**Carrot**   Fifty thousand dwarfs now, sir. *And* there's some dispute over the choice of king. Rhys Rhysson is a modern thinker, although he doesn't like Ankh-Morpork much.

**Vimes**   Sounds like a clear thinker to me.

**Carrot**   The more traditional dwarfs thought the next king should have been Albrecht Albrechtson.

**Vimes**   Who is *not* a modern thinker?

**Carrot**   He even thinks living above ground is dangerously non-dwarfish.

**Cheery Littlebottom** *enters, hurriedly.*

**Cheery Littlebottom**   Commander! Captain!

**Vimes**   Cheery? What is it?

**Cheery Littlebottom**   A robbery, sirs. At the Dwarf Bread Museum . . .

**Carrot**   Not . . . ?

**Cheery Littlebottom**   Yes, sir. It's the Scone of Stone. It's gone!

**Gaspode**   Corporal Cheery Littlebottom now pronounces her first name as Cheri. She is the first dwarf to openly admit to being anything other than 'he'. It's not that dwarfs aren't interested in sex, you understand; it's just that they don't see any point in distinguishing between the sexes anywhere but in private. Wouldn't suit dogs, that. The dwarfs just don't have a female pronoun, or any conception of 'women's work'. At least, not once the children are on solids anyway. When Cheery, sorry, Cheri arrived in Ankh-Morpork she found that there were 'men' who did not wear chain mail and *did* wear interesting colours and make-up. She found that they were called 'women' and she thought, 'If they can do it, why not me?' This has caused great controversy amongst the other dwarfs. You know – parents worrying that their sons might turn out to be daughters. Cheri still wears her beard, of course – it's one thing to declare yourself to be female, but it would be quite unthinkable to declare that you weren't a *dwarf*.

**Vimes** *and* **Cheery** *move into the museum. There is a podium centre stage. It is unoccupied, apart from a handwritten label: 'THE SCONE OF STONE (replica)'.* **Detritus** *is on guard by it.*

**Vimes**    First time I've been in the Dwarf Bread Museum. Thank you, sergeant. Guard the door and stop anyone entering, would you?

**Detritus**    Sir!

*He exits.*

**Cheery Littlebottom**    Open and shut case, sir. The Scone's gone and there don't seem to be any clues.

**Vimes**    No dropped fag ends, wallets or bits of paper with an address on them?

**Cheery Littlebottom**    No, sir. They were inconsiderate thieves.

**Vimes**    But what's the point? It's just a replica . . . I suppose you might swap it with the real thing.

**Cheery Littlebottom**    Yes, sir, but the replica is only made of plaster, sir. And it has a big cross carved on its underside. Good idea, apart from that, sir. And of course the real Scone is very heavily guarded. It's very rare that most dwarfs get a chance to see it.

**Vimes**    So. Why bother? You OK about this trip to Überwald, Cheery?

**Cheery Littlebottom**    Oh, yes sir. Got to face it sometime.

**Vimes**   I've been trying to bone up on dwarf lore, but I'm going to make lots of mistakes.

**Cheery Littlebottom**   I shouldn't worry, sir. Humans always do. But dwarfs can spot if you're trying not to make them.

**Vimes**   I mean, for one thing, there's all this fuss about a female dwarf trying to act like a . . .

**Cheery Littlebottom**   A lady, sir?

**Vimes**   Yeah, but no-one queries Carrot being called a dwarf, but he's human . . .

**Cheery Littlebottom**   No, sir. Like he says, he's a dwarf. He was adopted by dwarfs. He's performed the Y'grad (*eegrad*), he observes the j'kargra (*jacar-grar*) as far as it's possible in a city. He's a dwarf.

**Vimes**   But he's over six foot tall.

**Cheery Littlebottom**   He's a tall dwarf. Anyway, most of the Ankh-Morpork dwarfs are quite liberal, sir. They get along with humans. But some of the Überwald dwarfs, well, let's say they don't get out much. They say that Albrecht Albrechtson's never seen sunlight in his entire life. Everyone was certain he'd be elected king.

**Vimes**   But he wasn't. Of course, a lot of Ankh-Morpork dwarfs were *born* here. The world's moved on. They didn't want to be told what to do by an old dwarf sitting on a stale bun under a distant mountain.

**Cheery Littlebottom**   That's about it, sir, yes.

**Vimes** (*pensively*)   But why me? The city's lousy with diplomats. They know all the right nods and winks. Vetinari is throwing me to the wolves.

**Cheery Littlebottom**   And the dwarfs, sir. And the vampires.

**Vimes**    Yes, very good. Thank you, Corporal. You can report back to the Watch House. Ask Sergeant Detritus to come in as you leave, would you?

**Cheery Littlebottom**    Yes, sir.

*She exits. A moment and* **Detritus** *enters.*

**Detritus**    You wanted to see me, sir?

**Vimes**    Yes, Sergeant. How do *you* feel about going back to the old country?

*A pause.* **Detritus** *has not understood.* **Vimes** *prompts him.*

Überwald, I mean.

**Detritus**    Dunno, sir. I was just a pebble when we left there. Dad wanted a better life in der big city.

**Vimes**    There'll be a lot of dwarfs there. I know that dwarfs and trolls have a long history of fighting.

**Detritus**    No problem, sir. I'm very modern about dwarfs.

**Vimes**    These might be a bit old-fashioned about you, though.

**Detritus**    You mean them deep-down dwarfs?

**Vimes**    There's still wars up near the Hub, I hear. Tact and diplomacy will be called for.

**Detritus**    You have come to the right troll for dat, sir.

**Vimes**    Good. See you tomorrow, then. Oh, I need to speak to Angua, too. Where is she?

**Detritus**    Haven't seen her, sir. I'll put messages out for her.

**Vimes**    Thank you.

*Blackout.*

## Scene Three

*Vimes's and Sybil's house. The two of them are sat on stage.*
**Lady Sybil** *is knitting/sewing.* **Vimes** *is reading a
newspaper/book, distractedly.*

**Sybil**    I will tell Willikins to pack winter clothes. It's cold
in Überwald this time of year.

**Vimes** (*not really listening*)    That's a good idea.

**Sybil**    We'll need to host a party at the Embassy. We'd
better take some Ankh-Morpork food. Fly the flag. Should I
take a cook, do you think?

**Vimes**    Yes, dear. No-one outside the city knows how to
make a proper knuckle sandwich.

**Sybil**    Should we take the privy with us, do you think?

**Vimes**    Yes, that might be advisable . . . Privy? What for?

**Sybil**    You were miles away, Sam. Überwald, I expect.

**Vimes**    Sorry.

**Sybil**    Is there a problem?

**Vimes**    Why's he sending *me*?

**Sybil**    I'm sure Havelock shares with me the conviction
that you have hidden depths, Sam.

**Vimes**    Policemen don't go on holiday, Sybil. He knows
that. Where you get policemen, you get crime. If I go to
Bonk, Byonk, whatever, there *will* be a crime.

**Sybil**    It'll be nice to see Serafine again.

*Vimes's brow wrinkles.*

Serafine von Überwald. Sergeant Angua's mother? I told
you last year, Sam; we were at finishing school together. I
write to her every Hogswatch. A very old werewolf family.

**Vimes** (*absently*)    A good pedigree.

**Sybil**    Now you know you wouldn't like Sergeant Angua to hear you say that. Don't worry so. It'll give you a chance to relax. It will be like a second honeymoon.

**Vimes**    I don't think we ever actually got round to the first one, Sybil.

**Sybil**    No. But on that subject, Sam . . . I was talking yesterday to old Mrs Content, and . . .

**Willikins** *enters, followed by* **Inigo Skimmer**

**Willikins** (*clearing his throat*)    A gentleman to see you, your grace.

**Sybil**    Oh, well, I expect it's important. I'll leave you to it. We can talk later.

*She exits with* **Willikins** *as* **Skimmer** *moves towards* **Vimes**.

**Inigo Skimmer**    I'm so sorry to disturb your grace.

**Vimes**    Not your grace. Just Vimes. Sir Samuel if you must. Are you Vetinari's man?

**Inigo Skimmer**    Inigo Skimmer, sir.

**Skimmer** *makes a noise somewhere between a nervous laugh and a clearing of the throat. When he does this, it will be shown as 'mhm-mhm'.*

I am to travel with you to Überwald.

**Vimes**    Ah, you're the clerk who's going to do all the whispering and nudging while I hand out the cucumber sandwiches, eh?

**Inigo Skimmer**    I will try to be of service, though I'm not much of a winker. Mhm-mhm.

**Vimes**    Well, you'll travel with Sybil and me in the Ramkin coach.

**Inigo Skimmer**    Oh, I couldn't do that, sir. I'll travel with your retinue, mhm-mhm, mhm-mhm.

**Vimes**   If you mean Cheery and Detritus, they're in with us. Willikins, the cook and Sybil's maid are in the other coach.

**Skimmer***'s face falls.*

Bit of a tough choice, eh? Tell you what, come along in our coach, but we'll give you a hard seat and patronise you from time to time.

**Inigo Skimmer**   I'm afraid you're making a mockery of me, Sir Samuel, mhm-mhm.

**Vimes**   No, but I may be assisting. Now, if you'll excuse me . . .

**Willikins** *enters and coughs.* **Carrot** *enters discreetly behind him.*

Yes, Willikins?

**Willikins**   Captain Carrot to see you, sir.

**Vimes**   Thank you. Would you mind, Mr Skimmer? Watch business, you know. Nice to have met you, Mr Skimmer. I look forward to working with you.

**Inigo Skimmer**   Likewise, I'm sure, Sir Samuel.

**Willikins** *and* **Skimmer** *exit.* **Carrot** *crosses to* **Vimes***.*

**Vimes**   Yes, Captain?

**Carrot**   A murder, sir. Tradesman called Wallace Sonky. Found in one of his own vats with his throat cut.

**Vimes**   Vats?

**Carrot**   Of rubber, sir.

**Vimes**   Rubber vats? Wouldn't he just bounce out?

**Carrot**   No, sir, the rubber is in liquid form in the vat.

**Vimes**   Oh right. Of course, yes, you make things by dipping them into the rubber. Gloves, boots, that sort of thing?

**Carrot**   Er . . . that sort of thing, yes, sir. In fact, we got a pretty good rubber mould from Mr Sonky once we'd pulled him out and the rubber'd dried.

**Vimes**   Hold on. Sonky? Sonky? Carrot, are we talking Sonky as in 'a packet of sonkies, please, barber'?

**Carrot** (*very embarrassed*)   Yes, sir!

**Vimes**   So what was he dipping in the vat when his throat was cut?

**Carrot**   Nothing, sir. He was thrown in afterwards, it seems. Hr-rm.

**Vimes**   But he's practically a national hero!

**Carrot**   Sir?

**Vimes**   Well, the housing shortage in Ankh-Morpork would be a damn sight worse if it wasn't for poor old man Sonky and his penny-a-packet preventatives. Dear, oh dear. Anything else?

**Carrot**   Have you seen Sergeant Angua, sir?

**Vimes**   Me? No. I was expecting her to be travelling with us to Überwald. Something wrong?

**Carrot**   She didn't turn up for duty last night. It wasn't the full moon so it's a bit . . . odd. Nobby said she seemed a bit distracted when he was on duty with her the other day.

**Vimes**   You've checked her digs?

**Carrot**   Her bed's not been slept in. Nor her basket.

**Vimes**   Well, I can't help you, Carrot. After all, she's your girlfriend.

**Carrot**   She's been a bit worried, sir. About the future.

**Vimes**   What, the werewolf thing?

**Carrot** (*nodding*)   It preys on her mind, I think.

**Vimes**   Well, perhaps she's just gone somewhere to think over things.

**Carrot**   I hope so, sir. It's quite stressful. Being a werewolf in the big city. But I'm sure we'd have heard if she was in any trouble.

**Lady Sybil** *enters.*

Evening, my lady.

**Sybil**   Good evening, Carrot.

**Vimes**   Well, we'll just have to go without her. But keep me in touch, captain. The new semaphore towers go all the way to Überwald now, don't they?

**Carrot** *nods.*

A fake Scone goes missing a few weeks before a dwarf coronation and now a senseless murder. I'd like to be kept informed, right?

**Carrot**   Yes, sir!

*He exits.*

**Sybil**   Problems?

**Vimes**   Angua seems to have gone into hiding.

**Sybil**   Poor girl. The city's not really the place for her.

**Vimes**   Well, you couldn't winkle Carrot out of it with a big pin. And that's the problem, I suppose.

**Sybil**   Part of it, yes.

**Sybil/Vimes**   Children.

*Blackout.*

**Gaspode** *enters into a spot. In front of him is a little cap and a placard: 'Plese HelP This LiTTle doGGie'.*

**Gaspode**   Sometimes it seems to old Vimesey here that everyone knew that Carrot was the rightful heir to the vacant throne of Ankh-Morpork. But Carrot just wanted to be a copper, and everyone went along with it. Kingship, though, is a bit like a grand piano – you can put a cover over it, but you can still see what shape it is underneath. Vimes wasn't sure what you got when a human and a werewolf had kids. Perhaps just someone who had to shave twice a day around full moon and liked chasing carts. Compared with some of the city's past kings that'd be quite normal. But not everyone would see it that way. Maybe that's what Angua had gone to think about. We'll see. Maybe that's what she said in the note delivered to Carrot by carrier pigeon. A very tired carrier pigeon. Must have flown for quite some way. Obviously bothered him, 'cos he resigned from the Watch and set out on a search for the city's best tracker dog . . .

*More lights come up. Someone walks past and drops in a coin. Another walks over and reads the placard.* **Gaspode** *whines appealingly. The person drops a washer into the cap and then starts to exit.*

**Gaspode** (*examining the washer*)    A bloody washer?

*Calling after the donor.*

And I hope your leg falls off, ya bastard.

*The person turns and looks back at* **Gaspode**.

Woof?

*The person looks puzzled and then exits.*

Yeah – woof woof bloody woof. Right, then. This is me joining the plot now.

**Carrot** *enters.*

**Carrot**    Ah, Gaspode. I need your help.

**Gaspode**    Not me. I don't help the Watch. Nothin' personal, but it ruins my street cred.

**Carrot**    I'm not talking about helping the Watch. This is personal.

*He pats* **Gaspode**'s *head.*

I need your nose.

*He wipes his hand on his tunic.*

Unfortunately, this means I need the rest of you as well but I know that underneath that itchy exterior there beats a heart of gold.

**Gaspode**    Nothing good ever starts with 'I need your help'.

**Carrot**    It's Angua.

**Gaspode**    Oh dear.

**Carrot**    I want you to track her.

**Gaspode**    Werl, not many dogs can track a werewolf. They're cunning, see?

**Carrot**    Always go to the best, I always say.

**Gaspode**    Where's she headed?

**Carrot**    Überwald.

**Gaspode**    What? That's hundreds of miles away! And dog miles is seven times longer! Not a chance!

**Carrot**    Oh? Right then. Silly of me to suggest it. You're right. It's ridiculous.

**Gaspode** (*slightly suspicious*)    I didn't say it was ridiculous. I just said it was hundreds of miles away.

**Carrot**    You're a smart dog. Always said so. World's only talking dog, too.

**Gaspode**    Keep your voice down! Überwald's wolf country. I could've been a wolf you know?

**Carrot**    Oh yes?

**Gaspode**    With diff'rent parents, o' course.

*Pause.*

Steak?

**Carrot**    Every night.

**Gaspode**    You're on.

*Blackout.*


## Scene Four

*An inn.* **Inigo Skimmer** *is on stage, sat on a stool eating a sandwich.* **Vimes** *enters, carrying a napkin.* **Skimmer** *stands.*

**Inigo Skimmer**    Ah, your grace. I trust you have eaten well?

*As* **Vimes** *delivers the next speaks, he dabs absently at his mouth with the napkin. Unseen by him,* **Willikins** *silently enters.*

**Vimes**    Yes. But it irritates me the way Willikins gets to these inns a couple of hours before we do, commandeers the dining room and installs our cook in the kitchen. I hate this sort of thing, Skimmer.

**Willikins** *is standing beside* **Vimes**. *Unthinkingly, and without really being aware of* **Willikins**'s *presence,* **Vimes** *drops the napkin into* **Willikins**'s *hand.* **Willikins** *exits.*

Rank and privilege. Being treated like royalty.

**Inigo Skimmer**    But you see, your grace, you're not here as an individual, but as Ankh-Morpork. When people look at you they see the city, mhm, mhm.

**Vimes**    They do? Then I should stop washing, should I?

**Inigo Skimmer**    That is very droll, sir. But you see, you and the city are one. If you are insulted, Ankh-Morpork is insulted. If you befriend, Ankh-Morpork befriends.

**Vimes**    Really? And what happens when I use the privy?

**Sybil** *enters.*

**Inigo Skimmer**   That's up to you, sir. Mhm, mhm. Oh, excuse me, my lady, I must see how things are progressing.

**Skimmer** *exits.*

**Sybil**   What was all that about using the privy, Sam?

**Vimes**   Oh, nothing. Bloody hell. If I cut my toast into soldiers, we're probably at war!

**Littlebottom** *enters.*

**Cheery Littlebottom**   Sir, we've had a reply to that semaphore message you sent back to Ankh-Morpork from last night's town. Oh, and the Scone from the museum's been found.

**Vimes**   Good.

**Cheery Littlebottom**   But Constable Shoe's worried about it, sir. He seems to think someone used Sonky's rubber vats to make a copy, sir.

**Vimes**   What? A fake of a fake? What good's that?

**Cheery Littlebottom**   Couldn't say, sir.

*She hands him the two messages.*

Er . . . your other surmise, about Mr Skimmer, sir, was correct, sir.

**Vimes**   Thanks, Cheery. We'll be down shortly. I expect we ought to be getting under way.

**Cheery Littlebottom**   Yessir.

**Cheery** *exits.* **Vimes** *reads the 'Skimmer' note and hums to himself.*

**Sybil**   Sam, you're humming again. That means something awful is going to happen to someone.

**Vimes** (*waving the note*)   Wonderful thing, technology. Messages travelling over great distances in just a few minutes. It really does have its uses.

*He grins.*

**Sybil**   And when you grin like that it means someone's playing silly buggers but doesn't know you've just thrown a six.

**Vimes**   Don't know what you mean, dear. It's just the country air agreeing with me.

**Sybil**   Sam?

**Vimes**   Yes?

**Sybil**   This probably isn't the right time to mention it, but I went to see old Mrs Content the midwife the other day. And she says that we . . .

**Skimmer** *enters.*

**Inigo Skimmer**   We should be leaving, your grace, if you don't mind. I would like us to be through the pass at Willinus before dark, mhm, mhm.

**Sybil**   Do we *have* to rush so?

**Inigo Skimmer**   Well, the pass is . . . slightly dangerous. Somewhat lawless.

**Vimes**   Only somewhat?

**Inigo Skimmer**   I'll just feel happier with the pass behind us, sir. It would be a good idea if the second coach stays with us closely and your men stay alert, your grace.

**Vimes**   They teach you *tactics* in Lord Vetinari's *political* office, do they, Inigo?

**Inigo Skimmer**   Just common sense, sir.

**Vimes**   Why don't we wait until tomorrow before attempting the pass?

**Inigo Skimmer**   With respect, your grace, I suggest not. For one thing, the weather is worsening. And I'm sure we are being watched. We must demonstrate that there is no yellow in the Ankh-Morpork flag.

**Vimes**   There is. It's on the owl and the collars of the hippos.

**Inigo Skimmer**   I mean . . . that the colours of the Ankh-Morpork flag do not run.

**Vimes**   Only since we got the new dyes. All right, all right, I know what you mean. But look, I'm not risking the servants' lives if there's any danger. They can stay here and take the mail coach tomorrow.

**Inigo Skimmer**   Yes, your grace. And I suggest Lady Sybil remains, too.

**Sybil**   Absolutely not. I wouldn't hear of it! If it's not too dangerous for Sam, it's not too dangerous for me.

**Skimmer** *opens his mouth to respond.*

**Vimes**   I wouldn't argue with her, if I was you. I really wouldn't.

*Blackout.*


**Scene Five**

**Gaspode** *is discovered in a spot.*

**Gaspode**   Vimesy's well on 'is way to Überwald, but me and Carrot are doin' quite well, too. Ace tracker, that's me. Bin pickin' up info from the howling, too. That's a sort of wolf semaphore. There's been a lot of howling about Angua. The wolves fink she's bad news. Wolves hate werewolves, see? Humans don't like werewolves; wolves don't like werewolves. Wolves don't like wolves that can think like people and *people* don't like people that can act like wolves. Bit awkward for Carrot, though. Angua's travellin' with a big he-wolf from Überwald. He's a bad news wolf, they say. Might get a bit tricky. Complicated animals, people.

**Gaspode** *sighs. Lights out.*

## Scene Six

*A mountain pass. Wind, snow. We hear the carriage approaching and halt. Then* **Vimes**, **Sybil** *and* **Skimmer** *enter.*

**Inigo Skimmer** *(pointing, off )*    There! That's the Willinus Pass. The storm's closing in. We shall have to hurry.

**Sybil**    Why?

**Inigo Skimmer**    The Willinus Pass will probably be closed for several days, my lady. If we wait, we may even miss the coronation. And . . . er . . . there might even be some slight bandit activity.

**Vimes**    *Slight* bandit activity? You mean they wake up and then decide to stay in bed? Or they just steal enough for a coffee?

**Inigo Skimmer**    Very droll, sir. They do, notoriously, take hostages . . .

**Sybil**    Bandits don't frighten me.

*A twig cracks, off.*

What was that?

**Inigo Skimmer**    I'll check.

*He exits.*

**Vimes**    Skimmer! Stay here! I'll check it out. Skimmer!

*Silence. A strangled cry.*

Skimmer!

**Chief Bandit** *(off )*    Your grace, Vimes! There are many of us. Put up your hands, please! We have disarmed your dwarf and your troll. You must pay to use the Willinus Pass.

**Vimes** *and* **Sybil** *comply.* **Vimes** *has his hands clasped behind his neck.*

Well done, your grace, Vimes.

**Vimes**   You all right, Sybil?

**Sybil**   Of course, Sam.

*The bandits enter, with* **Detritus** *and* **Cheery**.

**Cheery Littlebottom**   Sorry, Commander.

**Vimes** *waves 'don't worry'.*

**Chief Bandit**   Keep your hands where I can see them, your grace, Vimes.

**Vimes**   OK. You've got me. But are you going to promise you'll let her go?

*The* **Chief Bandit** *crosses to* **Vimes** *and speaks straight into his face.*

**Chief Bandit**   Now, your grace, why ever would I do that? I am sure that Ankh-Morpork will pay a lot of money for your return.

**Vimes**   Thought so. Sybil?

**Sybil**   Yes, Sam?

**Vimes**   Duck.

*Strobe on. In slow motion, as* **Sybil** *ducks down,* **Vimes** *brings out a dagger hidden in the back of his tunic and stabs the* **Chief Bandit** *in one movement. At the same time,* **Skimmer** *appears as if from nowhere and despatches the bandit guarding* **Cheery** *(and another one, if you have that large a cast).* **Detritus** *decks the guard next to him. If there are any left, they run off, pursued by* **Skimmer**.

**Cheery Littlebottom**   I think they've all gone, sir.

**Vimes**   Then we'd better join them. Detritus!

**Detritus**   Sir?

**Vimes**   You two take the other coach, Sybil and I can manage ours and let's get the hell out of here, right? You OK, Sybil?

**Sybil**   Yes, of course. I knew you'd sort it out. I wasn't a bit frightened.

**Vimes**   Really? I was scared shi . . . stiff.

**Sybil**   But where's Mr Skimmer?

*There is a scream, off.*

**Vimes**   Forget him. He's alive and well, which is more than you can say for those around him.

**Sybil** *is shaking.*

Sybil? Are you all right?

**Sybil**   Sorry, Sam. Letting you down like this. It was just a bit of a shock, that's all. They would've killed us, wouldn't they?

**Vimes** *is at a bit of a loss. He pats her shoulder, helplessly.*

**Vimes**   You just . . . I mean, Cheery will . . . and I'll, er. Cheery!

**Cheery Littlebottom**   Sir?

**Vimes**   Help Lady Sybil on to the coach, would you? I just want to check something out here.

**Cheery Littlebottom**   Yessir.

**Cheery** *helps* **Lady Sybil** *off, followed by* **Detritus**. **Vimes** *moves over to one side.*

**Vimes**   Skimmer?

**Skimmer** *emerges.*

I knew you weren't a clerk. Searched your bags earlier while you were, well, out in the bushes. Just confirmed what I already knew. You're an assassin, aren't you?

**Inigo Skimmer**   With a capital 'A', if you don't mind, mhm, mhm. Properly qualified member of the Guild, you know. I am here for your protection.

**Vimes**   Vetinari sent you, did he?

**Inigo Skimmer**   Really, you know we cannot divulge our clients' names.

**Vimes**   Bit bizarre, though. *Me* being protected by the Assassins Guild. Do you know how many of your lot have tried to kill me?

**Inigo Skimmer**   Yes, your grace. Nine.

**Vimes**   So – you've been sent here to protect me. Why do I need protection?

**Inigo Skimmer**   Well, your grace, here they don't play by the rules.

**Vimes**   I've spent most of my life dealing with people who don't play by the rules.

**Inigo Skimmer**   So I gather. But at least when you kill *them*, they don't get up again. Shall we go?

*He exits.* **Vimes** *follows. Lights out.*


**Scene Seven**

*A clearing in the woods in Überwald. Snow on the ground. Snow falling.* **Carrot** *and* **Gaspode** *are shivering by a small fire.*

**Gaspode**   They're so close I can smell them. They've been tracking us all day.

**Carrot**   There has never been a case reported of an unprovoked wolf attacking a human being.

**Gaspode**   An' that's good, is it?

**Carrot**   What do you mean?

**Gaspode**   Werl, of course us dogs has only got little brains, but it seems to me that what you just said is the same as saying no unprovokin' adult human being has ever lived to tell the tale, right? I mean, your wolf has only got to make sure they kill people in quiet places where no-one will ever know, yes?

**Carrot**    I wish you hadn't said that, Gaspode.

**Gaspode**    *You* wish I hadn't said it!

*Pause.*

What I miss is streets. I can be wise on streets. Know where I am on streets. I'm just dumb on mud and rock.

*A snore from* **Carrot**.

Hey! You can't go to sleep. If this fire goes out, we'll freeze to death. If we're lucky.

*Wolf noises, off.*

Werl, I suppose I could join *them*. Y'know – 'Come on, brothers, let us run together in the moonlight, but first let us eat this monkey' . . .  No, not gonna happen. That would be bad. Never been a Bad Dog. Bloody duty. It'll be the death of us dogs. Er, forget I said that.

*He calls to the wolves.*

Just passin' through! No trouble to anyone!

*Growling, etc., off. Some wolves enter.* **Angua**, *dressed as a wolf, is among them. She crosses to* **Carrot**.

So – have you had your holidays, yet? Hey – paws off, matey, he's mine!

**Angua's voice**    Actually, he's *mine*!

**Gaspode**    Angua?

*Blackout.*


## Scene Eight

*Outside the city gates of Bonk. We hear* **Vimes**'s *coaches approach and halt. There are two guards at the gates. Above is a hooded and* *cloaked figure (***Lady Margolotta***). To one side, a group of heavily-armed dwarfs stand chatting.* **Vimes**, **Sybil**, **Skimmer**, **Cheery** *and* **Detritus** *enter.* **Detritus** *is carrying his seige crossbow. The group of dwarfs immediately react when they see* **Cheery**.

**Vimes** *(as he enters)*   So. This is Bonk, is it?

*The dwarfs move over to* **Vimes**'s *party*.

Sergeant Detritus. Try not to look too troll-like.

**Detritus**   Tryin' like hell, sir.

**First Dwarf**   Tagrudzak?

**Inigo Skimmer**   Would you like me to take care of this, your grace?

**Vimes**   I'm the damn ambassador.

*He steps forward to speak to the* **First Dwarf**. *He clears his throat and then speaks.*

Kruz. Gradazak yad Vimes Duhkraha tokat brezdrog.

**Sybil**   Oh, well done, Sam. (*To* **Skimmer**.) What did he say?

**Inigo Skimmer** *(with a groan)*   He said: 'Good morning, I am Overseer Vimes of the Look. Let us shake our business.'

**First Dwarf** *(pointing at* **Cheery**)   Budan? Kraah! Dukraga *ha-ak*!

**Cheery** *looks shocked.* **Detritus** *moves to point his bow at the dwarfs. The dwarfs draw their weapons.*

**Detritus**   I know dat word he said to her. It is not a good word. I do not want to hear dat word again.

**Inigo Skimmer**   Well, this is jolly, mhm, mhm. If everyone would just relax for a moment, we might all get out of this alive.

*Vimes moves* **Detritus**'s *crossbow to a less threatening position.* **Skimmer** *draws the* **First Dwarf** *to one side. He has a lengthy mimed discussion, showing the dwarf several impressive documents from his satchel. We hear snatches of dwarf dialogue – including* **Skimmer** *making loud reference to 'Willinus Pass', at which point the dwarfs all turn to look in awe at* **Vimes**. *At length, the* **First Dwarf** *glares across at* **Vimes**, *makes a dismissive gesture and strides back over to his group, who then exit, muttering.* **Skimmer** *crosses back to* **Vimes**.

Well, that all seems to be sorted out. Miss Littlebottom was a bit of a sticking point. You'll appreciate that these are very orthodox dwarfs. A dwarf who is obviously female is an anathema to them. However a dwarf does respect very complicated and impressive documents. Something's up, though. He wouldn't say what, but they did want to search our coaches.

**Vimes**    The hell with that. What for?

**Inigo Skimmer**    He wouldn't say. I persuaded him we have diplomatic immunity.

**Vimes**    What did you tell him about me? What was that about the Willinus Pass?

**Inigo Skimmer**    They were very impressed at your prowess in single-handedly despatching those bandits.

**Vimes**    But I didn't . . . ?

**Inigo Skimmer**    A lot of diplomacy lies in appearing to be what you are not. You've made a good start, your grace.

**Vimes**    Oh, thanks very . . . . what? I see. Well, let's get on, then, shall we?

*He looks across at the gate guards.*

Ah, now we're on firmer ground. I think we're about to meet Sergeant Colonescue and Corporal Nobbski.

**Vimes** *leads the party across.*

**Vimes**   Well?

**Sergeant**   Pisspot.

**Vimes** (*without turning to look at* **Skimmer**)   Inigo?

**Skimmer** *moves forward.*

**Sergeant**   Kraznar yar Gvardia. Dobro Yootro.

**Inigo Skimmer**   The problem will be Sergeant Detritus. No trolls are allowed in the town without a passport signed by their owner.

**Vimes**   Detritus is a citizen of Ankh-Morpork and my sergeant.

**Inigo Skimmer**   However, he *is* a troll. Perhaps you could write a short note . . .

**Vimes**   Do *I* need a pisspot?

**Inigo Skimmer**   A passport. No, your grace.

**Vimes**   Then he doesn't, either.

**Inigo Skimmer**   Nevertheless, your grace . . .

**Vimes**   There is no nevertheless.

**Inigo Skimmer**   But it may be advisable . . .

**Vimes**   There's no advisable, either.

**Detritus**   I don't mind goin' back if . . .

**Vimes**   You're a free troll, sergeant. That's an order.

**Inigo Skimmer**   Your grace, the men are only obeying orders.

*He indicates a watching figure, above.*

We are being watched, sir.

**Vimes**   I'd noticed. Tell the guards, nice and loudly, (*he raises his voice, pointedly*) that the Ambassador from Ankh-Morpork commends them for their diligence. We're going.

There was an inn about ten miles back. We ought to make it before dark.

**Inigo Skimmer**    You can't go, your grace.

**Vimes**    We are leaving. What you do is up to you. Those men are carrying weapons made in Ankh-Morpork. Trade, Mr Skimmer. Isn't that part of what diplomacy is all about? I'm sure that our little watching friend is all too aware of that. Our people can go anywhere they like in this city or I don't go in. Get that passed on.

**Vimes** *returns to the group with* **Sybil**. **Skimmer** *crosses to the guards and has a frenzied conversation in mime. The guards look up to the hooded figure, who nods.*

**Sybil**    Well done, Sam. Serves them right, the little bullies.

**Vimes**    This is all just games-playing, Sybil. I know when people are playing silly buggers, 'cos I've done it myself.

**Skimmer** *crosses to* **Vimes**.

**Inigo Skimmer**    There will not be a problem with your requests.

**Vimes**    So I should think. I reckon I could get used to this diplomatic life. Come on.

*He salutes the hooded figure nonchalantly as he passes through the city gates, followed by the others.*

*Blackout.*


**Scene Nine**

*The woods.* **Carrot** *and* **Gaspode** *are sat by a fire.* **Carrot** *is dozing. To one side, a group of wolves are sitting or lying. One,* **Gavin***, is sitting staring at* **Gaspode** *and* **Carrot***.*

**Gaspode** (*to the audience*)    Ah. Morning. You find us well. Ol' Carrot was a bit close to death last night but 'e was saved by . . . well, by a blanket of wolves, really. Pack of them lay all around him to keep him warm. 'Course, he whiffs a bit now, but better to be whiffy than dead, right? The fire? Oh – Angua lit that. Even got the wolves to help. Amazin'. (*To* **Carrot**.) Time to wake up, I think.

**Carrot** *comes to as* **Angua** *enters.*

**Carrot**   *You* were tracking us?

**Angua**   No. The wolves were. They thought you were a damn fool. I heard it on the howl. And they were right. You haven't eaten anything for three days! Up here, winter doesn't creep in over a few months, you know. It turns up overnight! Why were you so *stupid*?

*They argue in silence as* **Gaspode** *turns to address the audience again.*

**Gaspode** (*to audience*)   Yes, well, this looks like shaping up into one of those human argument things, so I'll just leave them to it.

*He crosses to the wolves and sidles up to one of the females.*

Yo, bitch.

**Female Wolf**   *Vot* vas zat you said?

**Gaspode**   Er . . . hi foxy, um, wolf lady.

*She glares impassively.*

'Ello miss . . .?

**Female Wolf**   Vot *har* you?

**Gaspode**   Gaspode's the name. 'M a dog. That's a kind of wolf, sort of thing. So . . . what's your name, then?

**Female Wolf**   Go avay.

**Gaspode**   No offence meant. 'Ere, I 'eard that wolves mate for life, right?

**Female Wolf**   Vell?

**Gaspode**   Wish *I* could.

**Female Wolf** (*leaning right into* **Gaspode**'s *face*)    Vere I come from, ve *eat* sings like you.

**Gaspode**    Fair enough, fair enough.

*He starts to move back to* **Carrot** *and* **Angua**.

I don't know, you try to be friendly and this is what you get . . .

*As he nears* **Carrot** *and* **Angua**, *we start to pick up on their conversation.*

**Carrot**    . . . You might have told me.

**Angua**    You always want to understand things. It would've taken too long. Anyway, it's none of your business. This is *family*.

**Carrot** (*indicating* **Gavin**)    And *he's* a relative?

**Angua**    No. He's a . . . friend.

**Carrot**    Another werewolf?

**Angua**    No.

**Carrot**    Just a wolf?

**Angua** (*sarcastically*)    Yes. *Just* a wolf.

**Carrot**    And his name is . . . ?

**Angua**    He would not object to being called Gavin.

**Carrot**    Gavin?

**Angua**    He once ate someone called Gavin.

**Carrot**    What, all of him?

**Angua**    No, of course not. Just enough to make sure the man set no more wolf traps.

**Carrot** *tosses a stick at* **Gavin**, *which he catches (OK, OK, in his hands).*

**Carrot**    I'm sure we'll be friends.

**Gavin** *snaps the stick in two and then exits, slowly.*

**Angua**   Carrot? Don't do that again. He's not a dog. He's a killer. Don't look at me like that. I don't mean he eats grandmothers. I mean if he thinks a human ought to die, then they're dead. He will always fight. He's very uncomplicated like that.

**Carrot**   And he's . . . a friend.

**Angua**   Yes. (*In a sarcastic, sing-song voice.*) I was out in the woods one day and I fell into some old pit trap under the snow and some wolves found me and would have killed me but Gavin turned up and faced them down. Don't ask me why. People do things sometimes. So do wolves. End of story.

**Carrot**   Gaspode said wolves and werewolves don't get on.

*Exchanges of wolf howls.*

**Angua**   He's right. If Gavin wasn't here they'd have torn me to pieces. I can look like a wolf but I'm not a wolf. I'm not human either. I'm a werewolf, get it? You can't fool wolves. I can pass for a human with humans, but I can't pass for a wolf with wolves. Gavin's very persuasive; it was him who managed to get the wolves to help to build the fire. That's him now, negotiating our safe passage through the next territory. It's wolf politics.

**Gaspode**   Here, is he sayin' anything about us?

**Angua**   Yes. Yes, that bit was about you.

**Gaspode**   What did he say about me, then?

**Angua**   Small, horrible, smelly dog.

**Gaspode**   Ah, right.

**Carrot**   You said this is family . . .

**Angua**   I meant it's personal. Gavin came all the way to Ankh-Morpork to warn me. It takes a lot of nerve for a wolf to come into a city. It's got nothing to do with the City Watch. Or you.

**Carrot**    But I'm here now.

**Angua**    Go away. Please. I can sort this out.

**Carrot**    And then you'll come back to Ankh-Morpork?

*No reply.*

I think I should stay.

**Angua**    The city needs you.

**Carrot**    I've resigned.

**Angua**    What did Commander Vimes say?

**Carrot**    Nothing. He'd already left for Überwald for the coronation.

*It starts to snow.*

**Angua**    *He's* got mixed up in all this?

**Carrot**    Mixed up in what?

**Angua**    Oh, my family's been stupid. I'm not sure I know everything, but the wolves are worried. When werewolves make trouble, it's real wolves who suffer. People will kill anything with fur. Werewolves are smarter at escaping hunters. We're not nice people, Carrot. We're all pretty dreadful. But my older brother Wolfgang is something special. Mad, bad and dangerous to know. Father's frightened of him and so's Mother if she'd only admit it. He drove my other brother away and he killed my sister.

**Carrot**    How . . . ?

**Angua**    He *said* it was an accident. Poor little Elsa. She was a yennork. That's a werewolf that doesn't change. So was poor Andrei. Elsa always looked human. Andrei always looked like a wolf. But they were still werewolves; still in their genes. Elsa was harmless. When she was killed, Andrei ran off. He works as a sheepdog now. Wins prizes, so I hear

. . . Wolfgang's got to be stopped. He's plotting something with the dwarfs. Gavin's seen them meeting in the forest.

**Carrot**   I don't think I want to see you fighting.

**Angua**   Then look the other way! I didn't ask you to follow me. Do you think I'm proud of this? One brother who's a psychopath and another who's a sheepdog!

**Carrot** (*earnestly*)   A *champion* sheepdog.

**Angua**   You mean that. You really mean that. I have to sleep in a dog basket seven nights in a month and that really doesn't bother you, does it?

**Carrot**   You know it doesn't.

**Angua**   But it should. You're just so nice about it and a girl can have too much of nice!

*Pause.*

You really left?

**Carrot**   Yes.

*Pause.*

**Angua**   Oh. Well, you won't get far by yourselves now.

*To* **Gaspode**.

When did he last sleep? Properly?

**Gaspode**   Dunno, really, we've been movin' pretty fast, these last few days . . .

**Angua**   No sleep, no food, no proper clothing. Idiot! (*To* **Carrot**.) Rest for another hour. Then we'll be off. I hope you can keep up.

*Blackout.*

## Scene Ten

*The Ankh-Morporkian Embassy in Bonk. The stage is empty.*

**Igor** (*off*)    Welcome, welcome. Do come in. After you.

**Vimes**, **Sybil** *and* **Skimmer** *enter, followed by* **Igor**.

Good evening, marthterth, mithtreth. Welcome to Ankh-Morpork. I'm Igor.

**Inigo Skimmer**    Igor who?

**Igor**    Jutht Igor. I'm the odd-job man.

**Vimes**    You don't say.

**Sybil**    Have you had a terrible accident?

**Igor**    Well, I did thpill tea down my betht thirt thith morning. Kind of you to notithe.

**Vimes**    Where's the vice-consul, Mr Sleeps?

**Igor**    Gone, thir. Left rather urgently two weeks ago. Didn't thay where he wath going. Hathn't been theen thinthe. Ecthcuthe me, I'll jutht thow your men where to put the bagth.

*He scuttles out.*

**Sybil**    What a fine figure of a man.

**Vimes**    More than one, by the look of him.

**Sybil**    Sam!

**Vimes**    Sorry. I'm sure his heart's in the right place.

**Sybil**    Good.

**Vimes**    Or someone's heart, anyway.

**Sybil**    Sam, really!

**Vimes**    All right, all right. But you must admit, he does look a little . . . odd.

**Inigo Skimmer**   We need to get a good night's sleep, your grace. Tomorrow will be a busy day.

**Vimes**   Oh?

**Inigo Skimmer**   Yes, your grace. We have to present your credentials to the local bigwigs.

**Vimes**   Credentials?

**Inigo Skimmer**   Just letters from Lord Vetinari confirming your appointment, sir. The order of precedence will be the future Low King, then the Lady Margolotta and finally the Baron von Überwald. Each, of course, will pretend that you are not calling on the other two. It's called the 'arrangement'.

**Vimes**   Yes, I read the brief. Before the 'arrangement', in the old days of imperial Überwald, the whole show was run by the werewolves and the vampires and everyone else was just lunch, right?

**Inigo Skimmer**   Somewhat simplistic but broadly true, yes.

**Vimes**   But then the dwarfs got powerful, right?

**Inigo Skimmer**   Yes. So they drafted an arrangement. No-one would wage war on any of the others and everyone could live in peace. No garlic to be grown, no silver to be mined. And the werewolves and vampires promised that there would be no *need* for garlic or silver. Mhm, mhm.

**Vimes**   So – what're the dwarfs like?

**Inigo Skimmer**   The future Low King is considered pretty clever. Mhm.

**Sybil**   Rhys Rhysson? I believe he doesn't much like us.

**Vimes**   I thought it was Albrecht who didn't like us?

**Inigo Skimmer**   No, he's the one who'd like to burn Ankh-Morpork to the ground. Rhys merely wishes we didn't exist. The other two will be a lot easier to deal with. It may have been Lady Margolotta who was manipulating the guards when we arrived at the city gates, sir. She's a vampire.

**Vimes**  Oh. Does Sybil come with me for this bit?

**Inigo Skimmer**  No, your grace. Just you and your guards.

**Vimes**  Right, well Detritus will be staying here to keep an eye on her. What about you?

**Inigo Skimmer**  You won't need me, sir, they all speak Morporkian. In any case, I must look into the disappearance of our man Sleeps.

**Vimes**  If he's been killed – will that be an act of war?

**Inigo Skimmer**  Depends what he was doing, sir. Mhm, mhm.

**Vimes**  Ah. Spying, eh?

*He notices the trophy heads on the fourth wall.*

Good grief! I've never seen so many trophy heads in my entire puff. There must be hundreds.

**Sybil** (*also looking*)    Reminds me of my grandfather's study. But there's just about everything here . . . tiger, elephant, stag, (*she squints*) gerbil, I think, swordfish . . . oh no. Sam – look. It's a *troll's* head. What if . . . ?

*We hear voices as* **Detritus**, **Cheery** *and* **Igor** *return.*

**Vimes**  Quick! Stand in front of it!

*They try to mask it as the trio enter.*

**Detritus**  Something wrong?

**Vimes** *sighs and steps aside.*

**Vimes**  I'm sorry, sergeant.

**Detritus**  Oh. Yeah, dere used to be a lot of dat sort of thing in the old days.

**Sybil**   You don't mind?

**Detritus**   Well, it ain't *mine*, is it?

*He and* **Cheery** *exit with the boxes.*

**Vimes**   Igor?

**Igor**   Yeth, Ecthellenthy?

**Vimes** (*to* **Inigo**)   I'm an Excellency?

**Inigo Skimmer**   Yes, your grace.

**Vimes**   And still my grace as well?

**Inigo Skimmer**   You are His Grace His Excellency the Duke of Ankh-Morpork, Commander Sir Samuel Vimes, your grace.

**Vimes**   Don't some of those cancel each other out?

**Inigo Skimmer**   Strictly yes, but they set great store by titles in Ankh-Morpork, so it's best to play the full hand. Mhm, mhm.

**Vimes**   I was blackboard monitor at school once, for a whole month. Does that count?

**Inigo Skimmer**   Could be useful in the event of a tie-break, your grace. Mhm, mhm.

**Vimes** (*with an empty laugh*)   Ah, ha. Anyway, Igor?

**Igor**   We Igorth have alwayth preferred marthter. What wath it you were wanting?

**Vimes**   I want all this lot taken down as soon as possible.

**Igor**   Even the thwordfith?

**Vimes**   Even the swordfish.

**Igor**   The snow leopardth?

**Vimes**   Both of them.

**Igor**   What about the troll?

**Vimes**    Especially the troll!

*He and* **Sybil** *exit to their rooms.* **Igor** *looks up at the wall and sighs.*

**Igor**    Yeth, marther. (*To* **Skimmer**.) What thould I do with them?

**Inigo Skimmer**    Throw them in the river. I'll speak to Sergeant Detritus about the troll's head, though. He might want it to have a proper burial.

**Igor**    Yeth, thir.

**Inigo Skimmer**    And might it be possible to have some supper?

**Igor**    Yeth, thir, I've laid out thome bread and thauthageth, in the red drawing-room, thir.

**Inigo Skimmer**    And what's in the sausages?

**Igor**    Er . . . meat?

**Inigo Skimmer**    Fine, I'll give them a try.

**Igor**    Jutht along the corridor, thir.

*As* **Skimmer** *exits,* **Igor** *scuttles out and returns with a stepladder and a large screwdriver. With a sigh, he starts to mount the stepladder as the lights cross-fade to* **Vimes** *and* **Sybil** *in their room.* **Vimes** *is reading a book on Überwald,* **Sybil** *is sewing a button onto a shirt.*

**Sybil**    This place looks like the inside of a cuckoo clock. Oh, Cheery's volunteered to be my lady's maid for now.

**Vimes**    Oh, splendid.

*A very loud thump.*

Sounds like the elephant being removed.

**Sybil**    The floors are a bit chilly, though. Tomorrow I shall measure up for carpets. Thank you for getting rid of those awful trophy heads.

*They continue to read/sew. Thump, thump.*

Snow leopards.

**Vimes**   Both of them.

*Small thump.*

**Sybil**   Gerbil?

*Pause. Muffled scream, thump and a twanging noise, as of a ruler being twanged on a school desk.*

**Sybil/Vimes** (*after a heartbeat's pause*)   Swordfish.

*Blackout.*


**Scene Eleven**

*Snowy wasteland.* **Carrot**, **Angua** *lying under blankets. Wolves lying, asleep.* **Gaspode** *on-stage, awake in the snow (if the set change is a problem,* **Gaspode** *could just deliver this in a spot).*

**Gaspode**   Wotcha. Bloody cold, here. All right for them toffs in Bonk. *We're* picking our way through the barren wastes tryin' to get to Überwald and old *Vimesey* is strugglin' with issues like 'Is my b-a-t-h too hot?', 'Was there too much rice in that kedgeree?'. Tough at the top, innit? Anyway, Vimes's problems're just beginning, 'cos he's got to make the round of the local nobs – dwarfs, vampires and werewolves. Starting with a trip below ground to the dwarf kingdom. Bet it's nice and *snug* down there, though. Lucky basket!

*Lights cross-fade to* **Vimes** *and* **Cheery**.

**Vimes**   Look, you didn't really have to come, Cheery. I could've brought Detritus. Mind you, a *troll* in a dwarf mine might just cause more comment than a . . . well, than a . . .

**Cheery Littlebottom**   . . . Than a girl?

**Vimes**   Er, yes. This is all very impressive, though, isn't it? That room thing that moves from the surface down to here.

I hadn't realised that that dwarfs' underground was so . . . extensive.

**Cheery Littlebottom**    You handled the coach-searching well, sir.

**Vimes**    Diplomatic immunity, isn't it? Damn cheek. I can't work out what it is they think they're looking for, though. (*Pause.*) Where is everyone, then?

**Dee** *enters, followed by a small retinue of other dwarfs.*

**Dee**    Commander Vimes? Welcome to Schmalzberg. My name is Dee. You have papers?

**Vimes** *hands them over.* **Dee** *reads them.*

**Vimes**    Is there a problem?

**Dee** (*a little too abruptly to be convincing*)    No. No problem. We have *no* problems. It says here 'His Grace'.

**Vimes**    That's me.

**Dee**    And there's a 'Sir', too.

**Vimes**    That's me, too.

**Dee**    And an 'Excellency'.

**Vimes**    'Fraid so. I was blackboard monitor for a while, too.

*Muffled off-stage mutterings.* **Dee** *strains to listen.*

**Dee**    And what does a blackboard monitor do?

**Vimes**    What? Oh, I had to clean the blackboard after lessons.

**Dee** (*loudly, so as to be heard off-stage*)    Ah. Erasing the teachings when they were learned!

**Vimes** (*a little non-plussed*)    Er . . . yes.

**Dee**    A task given only to the trustworthy!

**Vimes**    Could be, yes.

**Dee** (*handing back* **Vimes**'s *letters*)   Well, these all seem to be in order. I fear the king is too busy to receive you at present.

**Vimes**   But I rather suspect that he knows all that has passed between us. Have you found the Scone of Stone yet?

**Dee**   How dare you? There is no possibility that the Scone has been stolen! This is a lie we would not want repeated! The Scone will be seen by all at the coronation!

**Vimes**   I merely . . .

**Dee**   Nor do we have to show the Scone to any prying troublemaker!

**Vimes** *keeps silent.*

It is well guarded. Everyone leaving the cave is carefully watched! The Scone cannot be removed! It is perfectly safe!

**Vimes**   So you *haven't* found it, then?

**Albrecht Albrechtson** *enters.*

**Albrecht Albrechtson**   Aranak Moraporak?

**Vimes**   Yes.

**Albrecht Albrechtson**   Kralnag grebnik prozdrik. Drotgrad zot bnadlig.

**Vimes**   Why, thank you. And may I . . .

**Albrecht Albrechtson** *indicates* **Cheery**, *who shuts her eyes and shivers in fear of the dwarf's reaction to her.*

**Albrecht Albrechtson**   Ha'ak!

**Vimes** (*to* **Dee**)   Who is this?

**Dee**   Albrecht Albrechtson.

**Vimes**   The runner-up? (**Dee** *nods.*) Then tell him if he uses that word again in my presence or in the presence of any of my staff there will be, as we diplomats say, repercussions.

**Dee**    Ghaldik Vimes hrag dignatz Ha'ak frod, trignod Willinus Pass braznee jod hva.

**Albrechtson** *has been bristling during* **Vimes***'s speech (which he clearly understood). He reacts, as do his attendants, to the reference to Willinus Pass, but as soon as the translation is over, he turns on his heel and storms out. A dwarf moves over to* **Dee** *and mutters in his ear.* **Dee** *turns now and speaks to* **Vimes***.*

The king will see you now.

**Rhys Rhysson** *enters, with a couple of attendants.* **Cheery** *bows.*

**Rhys Rhysson**    Thank you, young . . . er, dwarf. You may straighten up, look you.

**Vimes**    Are you the king-to-be?

**Rhys Rhysson**    Yes. Why?

**Vimes**    I was just expecting someone a bit more . . . kingly.

**Rhys Rhysson**    This diplomacy business. Getting the hang of it, are you, boy?

**Vimes**    I'll admit it doesn't come easy. I've not been trained for it, you see.

**Rhys Rhysson** (*under his breath*)    Grataz Bavnad. (*Aloud.*) I went to Ankh-Morpork when I was a child. 'Lawn ornament', they called me. And, what was it? Oh, yes . . . 'Shortarse'. I expect you'll tell me that sort of thing doesn't happen any more, does it?

**Vimes**    Well, it doesn't happen as often. You always get idiots who won't move with the times.

**Rhys Rhysson**    Ah, but you mean *Ankh-Morpork's* times, do you not? When people say: 'You must move with the times', what they mean is: 'You must do it my way'. You drain us of our best people. Then they have to live in squalor, look you.

**Vimes**   Can't really answer that, sir. But if I was king I'd wonder why people were happier living in squalor in Ankh-Morpork than staying back at home. Er . . . sir.

**Rhys Rhysson**   They come back to the mountains to die, though.

**Vimes**   But they *live* in Ankh-Morpork.

**Rhys Rhysson**   And now you want our gold, iron and fat. Is there *nothing* we can keep?

**Vimes**   Don't know, sir.

**Rhys Rhysson**   Your letters of accreditation have been noted. Good day, your excellency. Goodbye, Miss Littlebottom.

**Cheery** *looks stunned. The king smiles, briefly.*

Ah, the rights of the individual. The famous Ankh-Morpork principle, isn't it? Thank you, Dee, his excellency is just leaving. Give me a moment or two and then send in the Copperhead delegation.

*He turns and exits, followed by his guards.* **Dee** *and his retinue leave by another route.* **Vimes** *and* **Cheery** *now move out of that area and walk around the stage, to make their way to their interview with the vampire!*

**Vimes**   Seemed quite a decent sort.

**Cheery Littlebottom**   Yes, sir. Very . . . enlightened.

**Vimes**   What was that he muttered, when I said I hadn't been trained?

**Cheery Littlebottom**   He said, 'Who has?', sir.

**Vimes**   Thought so. It's not just a case of sitting on a throne and saying 'Do this, do that', then?

**Cheery Littlebottom**   Oh no, sir. Dwarfs are very argumentative. Of course, many wouldn't agree with that. None of the big dwarf clans are happy about all this – the

Copperhead dwarfs didn't want Albrecht, the
Schmaltzburgers wouldn't have anyone called Glodsson, the
Ankh-Morpork dwarfs were split both ways – and Rhys
comes from a small mining village near Llamedos that isn't
important enough to be on anyone's side . . .

**Vimes**  You mean he didn't get to be king because
everyone liked him, but because no-one disliked him
enough?

**Cheery Littlebottom**   That's right, sir.

**Vimes**   And who's next on our little list?

**Cheery Littlebottom**   The Lady Margolotta, sir.

**Vimes**   Ah yes. The damned vampire. Ah, here we are.

*They arrive at the castle and ring the bell. Immediately,* **Igor** *answers.*
*Same actor as before. Different '***Igor***'.*

Igor?

**Igor**   Yeth, marthter?

**Vimes**   What the hell are you doing here?

**Igor**   Er . . . I'm opening thith door, marthter.

**Vimes**   But why aren't you . . . ah. Sorry, I thought you
were Igor.

**Igor**   Oh, you mean my *couthin* Igor. Workth down at the
Embathy. How'th he doing?

**Vimes**   Er, pretty well.

**Igor**   Did he thay how Igor ith getting along, thir? Only
none of uth have heard from him for quite a while. Not
even Igor, and they've alwayth been clothe. Do come in,
thir, the mithtreth ith ecthpecting you.

**Vimes**   Are all your family called Igor?

**Igor**   Oh, yeth, thir. It avoidth confuthion.

**Vimes**   It does?

**Igor**   Oh, yeth, thir. Anyone who ith anyone in Überwald hath a thervant called Igor. I'll jutht announthe you. (*He clears his throat.*) Hith Grathe, Hith Ecthellenthy . . .

**Lady Margolotta** *bustles in. She is not traditionally dressed – she has on flat shoes, a tweedy skirt, a pink jumper and pearls.*

**Lady Margolotta**   Ah, Sir Samuel. How are you? I know you don't like being called Your Grace. Isn't this all tiresome? But it has to be done, I suppose.

**Vimes** *bows, a little awkwardly.*

Oh please don't bother vith all that. Vould you like a drink? Bull's Blood, perhaps?

**Vimes**   Is that that drink with vodka . . . ?

**Lady Margolotta**   No. I fear this is the other kind. Still, ve have that in common, don't we? Neither of us drinks . . . alcohol. I believe you vere an alcoholic, Sir Samuel?

**Vimes**   No, I was a drunk. You have to be richer than I was to be an alcoholic.

**Lady Margolotta**   Ah, vell said. I have lemonade, if you vish. And Miss Littlebottom? Ve don't have beer, you'll be glad to hear.

**Cheery Littlebottom**   Er, perhaps a sherry?

**Lady Margolotta**   Certainly. Igor? (**Igor** *departs.*) Isn't he a treasure?

**Vimes**   He certainly looks as though he's just been dug up.

**Lady Margolotta**   Oh, all Igors look like that. Extremely popular vith the young ladies, I gather. All Igors are. I find it best not to speculate vhy.

**Vimes**   You know a lot about me.

**Lady Margolotta**   Most of it good, I assure you. Although you're inclined to forget your papervork, you get exasperated easily, you are far too sentimental, you regret your own lack of education and distrust erudition in others, you are immensely proud of your city and you vonder vhether you might be a class traitor. And you loathe vampires.

**Vimes**   I . . .

**Lady Margolotta**   Qvite understandable. Ve're dreadful people, by and large. Anyvay – how did you like the king?

**Vimes**   He's very . . . quiet.

**Lady Margolotta**   Try cunning.

**Igor** *enters with the drinks.*

Ah, thank you, Igor. Vell, here's to your stay, Sir Samuel.

**Igor** *departs.*

**Vimes**   Thank you. You said the king was cunning?

**Lady Margolotta**   Did I? No, I don't think I could possibly have said that. It's not the diplomatic thing to say. I'm sure ve all support the new Low King, the choice of dvarfdom in general. Even if they thought they vere getting a traditionalist and got an unknown qvantity.

**Vimes**   Did you just say that last bit?

**Lady Margolotta**   Absolutely not. You know their Scone of Stone has been stolen?

**Vimes**   They say it hasn't.

**Lady Margolotta**   Do you believe them?

**Vimes**   No.

**Lady Margolotta**   The coronation cannot go ahead vithout it, you know?

**Vimes**   We'll have to wait while they bake another one.

**Lady Margolotta**   No. There vould be no more Low Kings. Legitimacy, you see. The Scone represents continuity all the vay back to Bhrian Bloodaxe. They say he sat on it vhile it vas still soft and left his impression, as it vere.

**Vimes**   You mean kingship passes from backside to backside?

**Lady Margolotta**   Humans believe in *thrones*, don't they? Crowns, relics, garlic. Anyvay, there vill be a civil war over the leadership which Albrecht vill surely vin, and he'll cease trading vith Ankh-Morpork. He thinks the place is evil.

**Vimes**   I *know* it is. I was born there.

**Lady Margolotta**   He has plans to declare all dvarfs who live there drarak.

**Cheery Littlebottom**   It means 'not dwarfs'.

**Vimes**   That's very big of him. I don't think that'll worry our lads.

**Cheery Littlebottom**   Um . . .

**Lady Margolotta**   Exactly. The young lady looks vorried. And you'd do vell to listen to her, Sir Samuel. How is Havelock Vetinari?

**Vimes**   The Patrician? Oh, fine.

**Lady Margolotta**   He must be qvite old, now.

**Vimes**   About the same age as me, I suppose.

**Lady Margolotta** (*suddenly ending the discussion*)   This *has* been an interesting meeting, Sir Samuel. I trust Lady Sybil is well?

**Vimes**   Er . . . yes.

**Lady Margolotta**   Good. I am so glad. Ve vill meet again, I am sure. Igor vill show you out.

**Igor** *has already appeared.*

My regards to the Baron, when you see him. Oh, but careful what you say, Sir Samuel. The verevolves retain a real doggie dislike to words like 'bath' and 'vet'; they're sensitive about it . . . it reminds them of their baser, animal side.

*She and* **Igor** *exit as* **Vimes** *and* **Cheery** *again walk out of the scene to make their way to the von Überwald castle.*

**Vimes**    What was all that about?

**Cheery Littlebottom**    Which bit, sir?

**Vimes**    Just about all of it. Why should Ankh-Morpork dwarfs mind if someone says they're not dwarfs?

**Cheery Littlebottom**    We'd be outside dwarf law. Marriages wouldn't be legal, old dwarfs wouldn't be allowed to be buried back home, contracts wouldn't be valid. Dwarfs like solid rules.

**Vimes**    *We* have laws.

**Cheery Littlebottom**    We prefer our own. If it happened, there'd be another war, sir.

**Vimes**    Another?

**Cheery Littlebottom**    The last one happened mostly underground. Most humans knew nothing about it.

*They have arrived at 'another' door.* **Vimes** *knocks and* **Igor** *(again) answers – same actor again, different* **Igor***!*

**Vimes** *('up to speed' on the* **Igor** *thing now)*    Ah, hello, Igor.

**Igor**    Good day, your ecthellenthy.

**Vimes**    Igor and Igor send their regards, Igor.

**Igor**    Oh, thank you. Thinthe you mention it, could I give your colleague a parthel to give to Igor?

**Vimes**    You mean the Igor at the embassy?

**Igor**    That'th who I thaid, thir. He athked me if I could give him a hand. *(Small pause.)* I've got it wrapped in ithe.

**Vimes**    Yep. No problem.

**Igor**   If you'd wait here, I'll let the Baroneth know you're here.

**Igor** *exits.*

**Vimes**   Did he say what I thought he said? Wrapped in ice? (**Cheery** *nods.*) Impressive castle. Rather dangerous-looking moat, though.

**Cheery Littlebottom**   Yes, sir. Fed from the Bonk river; running water, you see? Keeps the vampires away, sir. Discharges directly over the Schmalzberg Falls. Two hundred foot drop, sir.

*The* **Baroness** *sweeps in.*

**Baroness von Überwald**   Ah, your excellency! Isn't Sybil with you?

**Vimes**   Er, she's staying at the embassy today. Baroness Serafine von Überwald?

**Baroness von Überwald**   Correct. And you will be Sam Vimes. Sybil's letters are all about you. Can I get Igor to get you a drink?

**Vimes**   No, thank you.

**Baroness von Überwald**   You met the new Low King?

**Vimes**   This morning.

**Baroness von Überwald**   I believe he's having trouble.

**Vimes** (*feigning ignorance*)   What makes you think that?

**Baroness von Überwald** (*taken aback*)   I thought everyone knew.

**Vimes** (*disingenuously*)   Well, I've only been here five minutes. I probably don't count as everyone.

**Baroness von Überwald** (*uncertain of her ground*)   We . . . heard there was some problem.

**Vimes** (*rather enjoying playing the fool*)   Well, you know – new king, coronation to organise, I suppose.

**Baroness von Überwald**   Er. Yes. Of course.

**Vimes**   Angua is well.

**Baroness von Überwald**   Is she? Good. Ah, here is my husband.

*The **Baron** bounds in and grasps **Vimes**'s hand in a vice-like grip.*

**Baron von Überwald**   Hello! Hello! Good of you to come, hey? Heard so much about you! Greatest respect for Ankh-Morpork, eh?

**Vimes** (*in pain*)   Er . . . good.

*The **Baron** releases **Vimes**'s hand and throws himself into a chair. The **Baroness** gives a 'tach!' of disapproval.*

**Baroness von Überwald**   You'll have to take us as you find us. This has always been a very *informal* household.

**Vimes**   It's a very nice place.

**Baroness von Überwald**   The embassy is to your liking? We owned it, you know, before we sold it to Lord Ve . . . Lord V . . .

**Vimes**   *Vet*inari . . . ?

*Something in the **Baron**'s doggie ancestry reacts to the 'vet' word. The **Baroness**, too, winces slightly.*

**Baroness von Überwald**   I expect your people have made a lot of changes.

**Vimes**   Yes, I must say I was extremely impressed by the new *bath*room . . .

*The **Baron** yelps and cowers in his chair. The **Baroness** turns to cast him a vicious glare.*

We were so lucky to have the thermal springs. Sybil wants to go to take the waters at *Bad (pronounced 'Bart' . . . the town name means Bath Hot Bath)* Heisses *Bad* . . .

*More reaction. Physical from the* **Baron**, *almost imperceptible from the* **Baroness**.

**Vimes**   I'm sorry, am I saying something wrong?

**Baroness von Überwald**   My husband is a little unwell at the moment. I believe you are to present your credentials?

**Vimes**   Oh yes.

*He hands them over. The* **Baroness** *reads them.*

**Baroness von Überwald**   It's a mere formality of course. I mean, everyone's heard of Commander Vimes. I mean, no offence, but we were a little surprised when you were appointed by Lord Ve . . . by the Patrician.

**Vimes** (*mildly*)   Lord Vetinari.

*More reactions. The* **Baroness** *is getting a little tetchy.*

**Baroness von Überwald**   Yes. We were expecting someone a little more . . . experienced.

**Vimes**   Oh, I can hand around thin cucumber sandwiches like the rest of them. And I'm a dab hand at piling up little golden balls of chocolate.

**Baroness von Überwald**   And you are a policeman. We've always opposed a police force in Bonk. It interferes with the liberties of the individual.

**Vimes**   I suppose that depends on whether the individual in question is yourself or the one climbing out of your *bath*room window with the family *silver* in a sack.

**Baroness von Überwald** (*enough's enough*)   We must be keeping you, and I'm sure you have a lot to do. Igor will show you out.

*She nods to the* **Baron**, *who exits. As she starts to leave,* **Vimes** *speaks.*

**Vimes**    I'll tell Angua you were asking after her.

**Baroness von Überwald** (*departing*)    Indeed.

*She has gone.* **Igor** *enters with a hand-sized metal box, with signs of frost on the outside.*

**Igor**    Here we are, ecthellenthy.

**Vimes**    Thanks. I'll be sure to give it to Igor.

**Igor**    No, not Igor. *Igor*, thir.

**Vimes**    Yes. Right.

*They leave as the lights black out.*


### Scene Twelve

*The Embassy.* **Igor** *is on-stage, sitting in a chair, with an ice-pack to his head.* **Lady Sybil** *is tending to him.* **Detritus** *stands by.* **Vimes** *calls, off, 'Sybil? We're back'. A moment, and then he enters.*

**Vimes**    Sybil? (*He sees* **Igor**.) What's happened?

**Sybil**    Detritus went out to look for him and found him flat on the snow next to the coaches.

**Igor**    I went out to unload the foodthtufth from the other coach, thir. I'd only jutht opened the boot when the lightth went out. I mutht have thlipped, thir.

**Vimes**    Or someone hit you.

**Vimes** (*pulling* **Detritus** *to one side*)    All right, Sergeant, talk to me.

**Detritus**    Just a feelin', sir. But I don't reckon 'e tripped and fell, sir. Nuffin's missin' but the coach was in a bit of a mess, sir.

**Vimes**   I think he must have disturbed someone searching the coach. Who *packed* the coach?

**Detritus**   Dunno, sir. Do you fink someone hid something on the coach, sir? *Smugglin'*?

**Vimes**   Could be. Good thinking, Sergeant.

**Detritus**   Sir.

**Sybil** *crosses to them.*

**Sybil**   He tells me Igors heal very fast.

**Vimes**   They'd have to.

**Sybil**   Mr Skimmer says they're very gifted surgeons, Sam.

**Vimes**   Except cosmetically, perhaps. I think I'd like to find out what's going on at home. (*To* **Detritus**.) There's a semaphore tower about fifteen miles from here isn't there? (**Detritus** *nods*.) Right, well, I think that Lady Sybil and I will take a quiet ride in the country this afternoon.

*Blackout.*


**Scene Thirteen**

*The semaphore tower, fifteen miles from Bonk. It is snowing.* **Vimes**, **Sybil** *and* **Igor** *enter.*

**Vimes**   Well, this is the semaphore tower but something's wrong. Go back and stay in the coach with Igor, Sybil.

**Sybil**   What is it?

**Vimes**   I'm . . . not sure. (*To* **Igor**.) If anything happens, you're to take Lady Sybil back to the Embassy, right?

**Igor**   Yeth, marthter.

**Vimes** *draws his sword.*

**Sybil**   Sam!

**Vimes**   You never know. I won't be long – after all we've got to attend that bash at the Low King's, er, place tonight. Back to the coach. I'll be fine.

**Sybil** *and* **Igor** *exit.* **Vimes** *puts his head round the semaphore tower door.*

Hello?

*He goes in. We hear his voice, off.*

This is the Watch. No, no it isn't you silly sod. Badge is no good out here.

*He enters at the top of the tower.*

No-one here. But whoever worked here has left in a bit of a hurry – food on the table, fire laid, door unlocked. Hmm.

**Skimmer** *enters silently.*

**Inigo Skimmer**   Tricky isn't it, your grace. There's only me here. Mhm, mhm.

**Vimes**   Where's the crew?

**Inigo Skimmer**   That's one of the mysteries.

**Vimes**   Hold on, why are *you* here?

**Inigo Skimmer**   The last time Mr Sleeps was seen he was coming out here with a message.

**Vimes**   Right. You said, 'One of the mysteries' . . . ?

**Inigo Skimmer**   The semaphore control arms have been completely smashed. Several hours work by skilled men would be needed to get them working again. I'd say the operators were forced to leave, mhm, mhm. In some disorder. There are wolf tracks outside, but then there are wolf tracks everywhere around these woods, sir.

**Vimes**   But the towers are fortified!

**Inigo Skimmer**   I know the company has rules, but you know what people are like. The trap up to the tower here *should* be bolted from above, sir. It wasn't.

**Vimes**   Needn't have got in from below, though. Could've landed on the top of the tower . . .

**Inigo Skimmer**   A vampire, you mean? There's no blood, but it's a thought.

**Vimes** (*picking up a couple of spherical grenades*)   Mortar bombs. (*Reading one of them.*) 'Badger and Normal, Ankh-Morpork. Mortar bomb. Red.' They're distress flares.

**Inigo Skimmer**   If there's a problem, they're supposed to fire one so that the next tower can send some men and a bigger squad can come from the nearest town.

**Vimes**   We need this tower working. I don't like being stuck out here without means of communication. We'd better fire one.

**Inigo Skimmer**   Best to wait until night, sir. That way more than the closest tower will see it. We don't know that there'll *be* anyone in the nearest towers.

**Vimes**   Good grief! You don't think . . . ?

**Inigo Skimmer**   I don't think, sir, I'm a civil servant. I advise other people, mhm, mhm. My advice is that an hour or two won't hurt too much. You should return with Lady Sybil. You have that dwarf reception to attend in any case. That is important, too. *Now*, sir.

**Vimes**   Very well.

*He departs.*

**Inigo Skimmer** (*calling after him*)   I will send up a flare as soon as it's dark and make my way back to the embassy. (*As* **Vimes** *appears at ground level again.*) I'll be safe enough.

**Vimes**   The *crew* weren't.

**Igor** and **Sybil** *re-enter.*

**Inigo Skimmer**    They weren't me, mhm, mhm. For the sake of Lady Sybil I advise you to leave *now*.

**Vimes**    All right.

**Skimmer** *moves out of sight.*

Right. Let's get going.

**Igor**    Ecthellent! A ruth to get home by thunthet! Jutht like the old dayth.

*He scampers off.*

**Sybil**    What happened?

**Vimes**    Don't know. It's not being able to do anything that's so frustrating. Everyone's hiding something. New king thinks I'm a fool, werewolves treat me like something the cat dragged in . . . The only one who's been halfway civil is a damn vampire!

**Sybil**    Not the cat.

**Vimes**    What?

**Sybil**    Werewolves hate cats. Not cat people. Another of those 'doggy' things, I suppose.

**Vimes**    Yes. (*He chuckles ironically.*) I reckon if I threw a stick for the Baron he'd leap out of his chair to catch it.

**Sybil**    Sam, I ought to tell you about the excitement about the carpets . . .

**Vimes**    What?

**Sybil**    The measurements at the embassy didn't work out properly. There was a secret room. A secret way in and out of the embassy. There's a sort of laboratory with various fat samples, lots of notebooks, a cupboard full of make-up and false moustaches . . . and this.

*She holds up a rather battered-looking journal.*

Maps, drawings, stuff about where the good deposits of fat are . . . oh, and listen to this: 'A werewolf putsch is clearly planned in the chaos following the loss of the Scone of Stone . . . K reports that many of the young werewolves now follow W, who has changed the nature of the game.'

**Vimes**   Spying. No wonder Vetinari always seems to know so much.

*He takes the book and looks at it.*

**Sybil**   Did you think it all came to him in dreams, Sam?

**Vimes**   This is useful. Come, we'd better get underway before Igor decides to race the sunset without us.

*They have exited. Lights cross-fade to* **Skimmer** *on the tower. He has set up the mortar and is trying to light the fuse on one of the bombs, but his matches won't strike.*

**Inigo Skimmer**   Damn. Mhm, mhm.

*There is a knocking at the trapdoor.*

Hello . . . ? Commander?

*He moves off-stage as the lights black out.*


**Scene Fourteen**

*The dwarf mine again. Noises, off, of a party in full swing.* **Vimes**, **Sybil**, **Cheery** *and* **Detritus** *enter.* **Cheery** *is wearing a real frock (red would be good), with a small 'cocktail' axe.* **Detritus** *has on bits of evening dress. As they enter and are greeted by a dwarf flunky,* **Dee** *rushes on and waves the flunky away.*

**Dee**   Your grace!

**Vimes**   Ah. Let me introduce my wife, the Duchess of Ankh-Morpork.

**Dee**    Er . . . or, um, yes. Er, delighted. I'm sorry, your grace, but could I just borrow your husband? Matters of state. My colleague will escort you to the reception.

**Vimes**    Detritus will stay with you, my dear. Cheery will stay with me.

**Sybil** *sweeps out, followed by* **Detritus** *and the flunky.*

**Dee**    You brought a troll!

**Vimes**    He's an Ankh-Morpork citizen.

**Dee**    But we're at *war* with the trolls!

**Vimes**    There are more important things than trolls at dwarf parties.

*He leans in to* **Dee**.

So – found your scone, yet?

**Dee** (*with a shifty glance from side to side*)    Come with me.

**Vimes**    Am I being taken to see something?

**Dee**    No, excellency, you are going to see something which is *not*.

**Vimes**    Then Cheery will join me.

**Dee**    *That?* Absolutely not! That would be a desecration!

**Vimes**    No, it wouldn't. She *won't* come with us because we're *not* going, are we? Officially? I mean, you wouldn't show the ambassador of a potentially hostile power that your political house of cards is missing a bottom layer, would you? Anyway, Corporal Littlebottom is the best scene-of-crime officer I've got.

**Dee**    Oh very well, then. She can come.

**Dee** *exits.*

**Cheery Littlebottom**    Where are we going, sir?

**Vimes**    Nowhere, Cheery. But Dee called you 'she'.
That's an improvement. Come on.

*They exit. The lights change to the Scone of Stone cave. Noise of a large
door being unlocked and opened.* **Dee***, followed by* **Vimes** *and*
**Cheery***, enter. Dripping water. Water effect. Blue lighting. There is
a slab on stage with (unlit) torches at each corner.*

**Vimes**    Is this it, then? A twenty-minute hike through
heavily-guarded and booby-trapped caves and a trip on a
lake and this is *it*?

**Dee**    Yes. This . . . is where *it* should be.

**Vimes**    Tell me what happened?

**Dee**    The Captain of the Candles found it gone when he
came down to change the wall candles.

**Vimes**    How often did he come in here?

**Dee**    Every day. But he is dead. He took his own life. I do
not think he could bear the thought of suspicion falling on
him.

**Vimes**    Could *he* have taken it?

**Dee**    No.

**Vimes**    How can you be so sure?

**Dee**    Watch me, your excellency.

*He walks back out of the room. A pause, then he returns.*

Now, just lend me your helmet.

**Vimes** *hands him his helmet.* **Dee** *again starts to walk out of the
room. Before he has gone more than a couple of steps, alarm gongs ring
and a guard rushes on. He salutes* **Dee** *and exits again.*

The mechanism is kept in perfect working order. It is
unavoidable and it is accurate to within a few ounces.

**Vimes**    Cheery. What do you see?

**Cheery Littlebottom**    Nothing much, sir. The room's carved out of solid rock and we've come in by the only entrance. The floor is covered in this off-white sand, but it's solid rock underneath.

**Vimes**    So. Only one entrance. Or exit.

**Dee**    The chamber is inspected regularly by myself and two guards.

**Vimes**    Where else is this off-white sand found?

**Dee**    Only in this cave. Is that important?

**Vimes**    Possibly. Tell me, what intrinsic value does the Scone have?

**Dee**    Intrinsic? It's priceless!

**Vimes** (*patiently*)    I'm trying to work out why a thief might want to steal it.

**Dee** (*pulling a letter out of his pocket*)    Perhaps this letter might help.

**Vimes** (*looking at it*)    It's written in dwarfish. (*He passes it to* **Cheery**.) What does it say?

**Cheery Littlebottom**    It's a ransom note, sir. From the . . . 'Sons of Agi Hammerthief'. They say they have the Scone and . . . they say they'll destroy it, sir.

**Vimes**    Unless?

**Cheery Littlebottom**    Unless Rhys renounces the kingship. There are no other conditions.

**Vimes**    Who are the Sons of Agi Hammerthief?

**Dee**    It's a made-up name.

**Vimes**    This isn't a real crime any more. It's politics. Who'll become king if he abdicates?

**Dee**    Albrecht Albrechtson, of course. The king is minded to step down. Better any king than chaos, he says. Dwarfs do not like chaos.

**Vimes**    Who *does*? Would you excuse us a moment? I need to have a few words with my corporal.

**Dee**    Very well.

**Vimes** *and* **Cheery** *cross to the opposite side of the stage.*

**Cheery Littlebottom**    Is it the sand, sir? Do you think the Captain of the Candles brought sand in under his clothes? To counterbalance the weight of the Scone when he took it out?

**Vimes**    Possibly. No-one expected anyone to try to steal the Scone. Those guards can't be alert all the time. I've done guarding. I know. I bet they're least alert just after an inspection. Someone fairly fit and nimble could swim across that lake and get in here unseen.

**Cheery Littlebottom**    Do you have an idea, sir?

**Vimes**    Possibly. (*To* **Dee**.) Did the Candle Captain come here at the same time every day?

**Dee**    Usually.

**Vimes**    So he *didn't*. When do the guards change?

**Dee**    Three o'clock.

**Vimes**    Did he go *before* or after they changed?

**Dee**    That would depend . . .

**Vimes**    So – if he went *before* they changed and *another* dwarf came *after* they'd changed, pretending to be him . . . ?

**Dee**    You think you know something . . .

**Vimes**    Let's say some ideas are forming, eh? Perhaps we should get back to the party.

*They exit as the lights change to the party scene. There is a large rustic chandelier above the stage; it looks heavy and wooden and has a lot of drippy candles on it. Guests – human and dwarf – stand around.* **Rhys** *is talking to a couple of guests USC.* **Lady Sybil** *is talking to* **Wolfgang von Überwald**. *He has his back to the audience. There are other werewolves among the guests.* **Vimes**, **Cheery** *and* **Dee** *enter.* **Wolfgang** *turns and comes down to him.*

**Wolfgang**    Ah, your grace, Vimes.

**Vimes**    And you are?

**Wolfgang** (*clicking his heels*)    Wolf von Überwald!

**Vimes**    Ah. Angua's brother.

**Wolfgang**    Yes, your grace.

**Vimes**    Wolf the wolf, eh?

**Wolfgang** (*solemnly*)    Thank you, your grace. That is very funny. Indeed, yes! It is quite some time since I heard that one! Your Ankh-Morpork sense of humour! Amusing puns and people dropping their trousers, yes?

**Vimes** (*indicating* **Wolfgang**'s *uniform*)    I don't recognise the regiment.

**Wolfgang**    We're more of a movement, really.

**Vimes** *doesn't react.*

There is a problem, your grace?

**Vimes**    What? No, I . . . just feel I've met you before somewhere.

**Wolfgang**    You called on my father this morning.

**Vimes**    Ah yes.

**Wolfgang**    Charming chandeliers in here, don't you think? Very . . . heavy.

*As* **Vimes** *looks up,* **Wolfgang** *drifts off back into the crowd.*

**Vimes**   Yes, they are . . . I . . . (*Sotto voce to* **Cheery**.)
Cheery, look.

**Cheery Littlebottom** (*also sotto voce*)   Sir?

**Vimes**   That chandelier. The one over the king.

**Cheery Littlebottom**   It's . . . moving, sir. The *king*,
sir . . .

*Strobe on. Everything goes into slow motion.*

**Vimes**   Your majesty! Look out!

*As the guests all turn to look up at the falling chandelier,* **Vimes**
*starts to run, in slow motion, across to* **Rhys**. *As he makes contact
with* **Rhys**, *pushing him to the ground, the lights black out. In the
dark, a noise of a tremendous crash. Screams.*

# Act Two

## Scene One

*A prison cell.* **Vimes** *is sat, in his shirt and trousers. Barred window gobo. Dripping water. He checks his pockets and pulls out a box of matches. He lies back on the bed and bangs his head on something under the pillow. He looks and it is a knife. He looks confused. There is a noise of a key in a door and* **Dee** *enters.*

**Dee**   Your grace? This is very unfortunate.

**Vimes**   *Why* am I in a cell? Is this some ghastly mistake?

**Dee**   Alas no. I am convinced of your innocence of course.

**Vimes**   Me too. In fact I'm so convinced I don't even know what I'm innocent *of*! I saved your king's life, for goodness' sake!

**Dee**   It has been suggested that you gave a *signal* just before the chandelier came down. Mr Skimmer was on your staff?

**Vimes**   Yes, but . . . look, let me talk to him.

**Dee**   He was found dead in the roof near the chandelier mechanism. We believe he became entangled in the winch mechanism when he released the chandelier. Three dwarfs were dead around him.

**Vimes**   He wouldn't have done that!

**Dee**   He *was* a member of your Guild of Assassins? We will investigate. The innocent have nothing to fear. Your dwarf and troll are under house arrest in your embassy. Your wife is with them. And then there is the other matter.

**Vimes**   What? You're going to accuse *me* of stealing the Scone?

**Dee**   You laid hands on the king.

**Vimes**   What? I didn't have much choice, did I?

**Dee**   You will remain as . . . our guest, while our investigations continue. I will return when I have news.

**Vimes**   This is ridiculous!

**Dee** *has exited. Noise of heavy door closing and being locked.* **Vimes** *sighs, heavily. He reaches under the pillow and brings out the knife.*

So. They took my sword and uniform. But who left me this dagger and why?

*Noise of key in lock. A dwarf comes in carrying a tray with a plate and glass.*

**Dwarf Guard**   Gruzdrak.

*He goes to put down the tray.* **Vimes** *suddenly punches him hard in the stomach, following it up with a swing to the jaw. The dwarf falls to the ground.* **Vimes** *picks up the knife and goes over to the dwarf.*

**Vimes**   *Someone* left me a weapon. They wanted me to kill you. Remember that. *I could have killed you.*

*He straightens up.*

Mind you, maybe they wanted *you* to kill *me.* If you want to help someone escape, you give them a *key.* Give them a weapon and they might just get killed in the effort . . . and there're bound to be more guards in the passage . . .

**Lady Margolotta** *enters.*

**Lady Margolotta**   Yes, Sam Vimes, but they are *not* conscious. Well, not any more.

**Vimes**   You! How did you get in?

**Lady Margolotta**   Dwarfs' minds are very easy to control.

**Vimes**   I *knew* you were behind all this!

**Lady Margolotta**   No you didn't. You knew the Scone vasn't stolen, though. I know you hate vampires. But if I vas you, I'd ask myself . . . do I hate them vith all my life?

**Vimes**   Just one bite will end all my troubles, eh?

**Lady Margolotta**   One bite would be one bite too many, Sam Vimes.

**Vimes**   'One bite too many?' *You're* a teetotaller, too?

**Lady Margolotta**   Just like you. Almost four years now.

**Vimes**   No blood at all?

**Lady Margolotta**   Oh yes. Animal. It's rather kinder to them than slaughter, don't you think? Of course, it makes them docile, but then the cow is unlikely ever to vin the Thinker of the Year award. I'm on a vagon, Mister Vimes.

**Vimes**   *The* wagon, we call it. And that replaces human blood?

**Lady Margolotta**   Like lemonade replaces vhisky. Come, I vill help you get out.

**Vimes**   Right!

*They exit as the lights black out.*


**Scene Two**

*Snowy wasteland. Wind. Snow. Night-time.* **Vimes** *and* **Margolotta** *enter (they've walked straight out of the prison set so these two scenes should follow each other without pause).*

**Vimes**   Where are we?

**Lady Margolotta**   In the mountains, qvite a long vay viddershins of the town, Mister Vimes. Goodbye.

**Vimes**   You're going to leave me *here*?

**Lady Margolotta**   I'm sorry? *You* vere the one who escaped. I am certainly not here. Me, a vampire, interfering in the affairs of dvarfs? Unthinkable! Let us just say . . . I like people to have an even chance.

**Vimes**   It's freezing!

**Lady Margolotta**   But you have *freedom*. Isn't that vhat everyone vants? Isn't *that* supposed to give you a lovely varm glow?

*She exits.*

**Vimes**   Wait, I . . . Dammit. What the hell time is it? Dusk? Dawn? *Shelter*. Shelter, that's what's wanted first and foremost. Best to head downwards, I suppose.

**Vimes** *starts to walk, on the spot, towards the audience. Wolves howl, off.*

Wolves? Who was it said they won't attack if you face them down?

*He trudges on. The lights fade out and come up again to indicate the passage of time.*

Damn, but it's cold. There must be some people around, surely? Charcoal burners? Woodcutters? Little girls taking goodies to Granny?

*He pauses and listens.*

Nothing.

*He trudges on. Lights go down and up again, indicating another passage of time.* **Vimes** *now looks much colder and more weary.*

What's that smell? Sulphur? Hold on, what did my briefing say? Something about natural hot springs bubbling from the rock? Mmm . . . *hot water* . . . oh, yes. Food can wait, thank you. Let's get into a nice hot bath, Commander. (*In* **Willikins***'s voice.*) 'I've run your bath for you, your grace. Blood heat, sir. Just as you like it.' Oh, Willikins, where are you when you're *really* needed?

*He arrives at a hot spring – steam/smoke rises from a hole in the stage.*

Ah!

**Vimes** *quickly strips to his long combs and steps in.*

Aaah! Oh, sheer bliss. Oh, yes. Hot water *is* civilisation.

**Wolfgang** *enters, followed by a few more werewolves.*

**Wolfgang**    Ah. Your grace . . . A run in the snow is very refreshing, no? You are certainly learning the ways of Überwald, your grace. Lady Sybil is alive and well and staying as our guest at the castle. I know you would wish to hear that.

**Vimes**    Why you . . .

*He pauses and makes the effort not to give* **Wolfgang** *the satisfaction of seeing that he's been rattled. He leans back in his spa.*

Nothing like a hot dip before breakfast.

**Wolfgang**    Ah yes. We also have not, as yet, breakfasted.

*The werewolves start to examine* **Vimes**'s *clothes.*

It is all a great game, your grace. The strongest survive, which is as it should be.

**Vimes**    Dee planned all this, did he?

**Wolfgang** (*with a laugh*)    The dear little Dee? Oh, he *had* a plan. It was a good little plan, if a touch insane. Happily, it will no longer be required!

**Vimes**    You want the dwarfs to go to war?

**Wolfgang** (*neatly folding* **Vimes**'s *clothes*)    Strength is *good*. But it only remains good if it is not possessed by too many people.

*He tosses the clothes to one of the werewolves.*

What is it you want me to say, your grace? Something like: 'You are going to die anyway, so I might as well tell you everything'?

**Vimes**    Well, it'd be a help. So, you expect me to die?

**Wolfgang**    No, Commander, I expect you to *talk*. You *are* going to die anyway. So why don't *you* tell *me* what you know?

**Vimes** (*happy to play for time*)    I'm pretty sure the replica Scone was stolen in Ankh-Morpork so that a copy could be made of it, which was smuggled here in one of my coaches. Diplomats don't get searched.

**Wolfgang**    Well done!

**Vimes**    Shame Igor came out to unload when one of your boys was there, wasn't it?

**Wolfgang**    Oh, it's hard to hurt an Igor.

**Vimes**    You don't care, do you? A bunch of dwarfs want Albrecht on the throne . . . on the *Scone*, because they like that old-time certainty and *you* just want dwarfs fighting. Albrecht won't even get the right Scone back, will he? And now you've set me up. Nice touch, leaving me that dagger. Old Dee must've really hoped I *would* kill to escape.

**Wolfgang**    Kill or be killed, yes? Is it not time you got out of that . . . pool?

**Vimes**    Oh, you mean this *bath*?

**Wolfgang** *and the others wince.*

Yes, you may be walking upright and talking, my lad, but something between a human and a wolf still has a bit of dog in it, eh?

**Wolfgang**    We have an ancient custom here. A little chase. The great game. Anyone can challenge us. If they outrun us, they win four hundred crowns. A tidy sum. Enough to start a small business. Of course, if they *lose*, the question of the money does not arise.

**Vimes** (*looking around for passing woodcutters or charcoal burners*) Does *anyone* ever win?

**Wolfgang**    Sometimes. If they train well and know the country. In your case we'd give you, oh, an hour's lead. For the sport of it! (*He points.*) Bonk is five miles in that direction. The custom says that you may not enter a dwelling until you get there.

**Vimes**    And if I don't run?

**Wolfgang**    Then it will be a very short event! We do not like Ankh-Morpork. We do not want you here.

**Vimes**    Strange that. Ankh-Morpork's *full* of folk from Überwald, all writing letters home saying, 'It's great here, they don't eat you alive for a dollar'.

*He pushes his luck a little further.*

Angua's doing well . . .

**Wolfgang**    *She* can't help you, mister civilised Ankh-Morpork! You *will* run!

**Vimes** *struggles out of the pool.*

You go into the water wearing *clothes*? (*To the other werewolves.*) Behold . . . civilisation!

**Vimes**    Four hundred dollars you say?

**Wolfgang**    Yes!

**Vimes**    What's that in *my* currency? About a dollar fifty?

**Wolfgang**    The question will not arise.

**Vimes**    Well, I don't want to have to spend it all *here*, do I . . .

**Wolfgang**    *Run!!*

**Vimes** *saunters off, with calculated nonchalance, but all too aware of the threat behind him. The werewolves sit in the snow around the 'pool'. Lights out.*

## Scene Three

*Interior of a dacha in the woodland. Three women in Victorian dress stand, looking out at the snow through a window in the fourth wall.*

**First Glum Sister**   How beautiful the snow is, sisters.

**Second Glum Sister**   And how cold the wind is.

**Third Glum Sister** (*with a sigh*)   Why do we always talk about the weather?

**First Glum Sister**   What else is there?

**Third Glum Sister**   Well, it's either freezing cold or baking. I mean, that's it, really.

**Second Glum Sister**   That's how things are in Mother Überwald. The wind and the snow and the boiling heat of the summer.

**Third Glum Sister**   You know, I bet if we cut down that cherry orchard we could put in a skating rink.

**First Glum Sister**   No.

**Third Glum Sister**   How about a conservatory? We could grow pineapples?

**First Glum Sister**   No.

**Third Glum Sister**   If we moved to Bonk, we could get a big apartment . . .

**Second Glum Sister**   This is our home, Irina. A home of lost illusions and thwarted hopes . . .

**First Glum Sister**   I remember when we lived in Bonk. Things were better then.

**Second Glum Sister**   Things were *always* better then.

**Third Glum Sister** (*with a gasp*)   There's a man running through the cherry orchard! He's heading here!

**First Glum Sister**   A man? What could he possibly want?

**Third Glum Sister** (*straining to see through the gloom*)    It looks like he wants . . . a pair of trousers.

**Second Glum Sister**    Ah . . . trousers were better then.

**Vimes** *bursts on. He has a sack clutched to him.*

Have you come to ravish us?

**Vimes**    Madam! I'm being chased by werewolves!

**Second Glum Sister**    And vill that take you all day?

**Vimes**    Ladies! Please, I need trousers!

**First Glum Sister**    Ve can see that.

**Vimes**    I would be so grateful. I may not look it, but I am His Grace the Duke of Ankh-Morpork . . .

*All three sisters sigh.*

**All Three Glum Sisters**    Ankh-Morpork!

**First Glum Sister**    Ve have alvays dreamed of going there!

**Second Glum Sister** (*aside, to the* **First**)    We *do* have the gloomy and purposeless trousers of Uncle Vanya.

**First Glum Sister** (*aside, to the* **Second**)    He hardly ever wore them.

*They scurry out.*

**Third Glum Sister** (*to* **Vimes**)    Do you have long, cold winters in Ankh-Morpork?

**Vimes**    Just muck and slush usually.

**Third Glum Sister**    Any cherry orchards?

**Vimes**    I don't think we have any, I'm afraid.

**Third Glum Sister** (*punching the air*)    Yes!

*The* **First** *and* **Second Sisters** *enter carrying some huge trousers as the lights black out.*

## Scene Four

*Elsewhere in the woods. Still snowing.* **Carrot** *and* **Gaspode** *are on-stage.* **Angua** *enters.*

**Carrot**   What did you see?

**Angua**   Wolfgang's got some poor devil playing the Game. I'm going to put a stop to it. It was bad enough with Father keeping up the tradition, but at least he played *fair*. Wolfgang cheats. They *never* win.

**Carrot**   This is the game you told me about?

**Angua**   Yes. If they won, Father gave them four hundred crowns and had them to dinner at the castle.

**Carrot**   If they lost he had them *for* dinner in the woods.

**Angua**   Yes. Thanks for reminding me.

**Carrot**   I was trying *not* to be nice.

**Angua**   You may have an undiscovered natural talent. But no-one *had* to run, is my point. I won't apologise. I've been a copper in Ankh-Morpork, remember? City motto: 'You May Not Get Killed'.

**Carrot**   Actually, it's . . .

**Angua**   I *know*! And *our* family motto is 'Homo Homini Lupus' – 'A man is a wolf to other men'. Humans hate werewolves because they see the wolf inside; *wolves* hate werewolves because they see the *human* inside – and *they're* right!

## Scene Five

*The woods. Snow, etc. Wolf howls.* **Vimes** *enters, looking hunted and wearing a very ill-fitting pair of trousers held up with string. He crosses to an exit, but it is blocked by a (were)wolf.* **Vimes** *sees a tree branch and picks it up to use as a weapon.*

*The werewolf stalks forward, but* **Vimes** *swings the branch round and catches it a mighty whack on the side of the head which knocks it to the ground. He moves swiftly in and administers another couple of blows. The werewolf slowly starts to rise again. Two other werewolves also enter from a different direction.*

**Vimes**    For God's sake, won't anything stop you?

*More wolf howls. Suddenly an arm appears wielding a sword. It is followed by the rest of* **Carrot**, *who stabs the wolf dead. The* **Angua** *werewolf (and* **Gavin***) also charges on and chases off the other two werewolves.*

**Carrot**    Bit of a close one there, sir.

**Vimes**    Carrot?

**Carrot**    We'll get a fire going.

**Vimes**    *Carrot?*

**Carrot**    I shouldn't think you've eaten.

**Vimes**    *Carrot!*

**Carrot**    Yes, sir?

**Vimes**    What the hell are *you* doing here?

**Carrot**    It's a bit complicated, sir. You seem to have lost your trousers, sir.

**Vimes**    Yes, it's the famous Ankh-Morpork sense of humour.

**Carrot**    We have your clothes, sir. Found them in the woods.

**Vimes**    Good. But where have the werewolves all gone?

**Carrot**    Angua and Gavin – and Gavin's people of course – have chased them off, sir.

**Vimes**    Gavin's people, eh? Well, that's good! That's very good! Well done, Gavin! Now . . . *who the hell is Gavin?*

**Gavin** *enters.*

**Carrot**   That's Gavin, sir.

**Vimes**   A wolf? I've been saved from werewolves by wolves?

**Gaspode** *enters and sits next to* **Gavin**.

And is that Gaspode? That mutt that hangs round the Watch House?

**Carrot**   Yes, sir. He helped me to track Angua from Ankh-Morpork.

**Carrot**   Yes, why *are* you here, Captain? I left you in charge . . .

**Angua** *(human) enters.*

**Angua**   Hello, Mister Vimes. They're miles away by now.

**Vimes**   What. Is. Going. On?

**Angua**   My family are trying to upset the coronation, sir. They're working with some dwarfs that don't want – that want to keep Überwald separate.

**Vimes**   I'd worked that out for myself, thank you.

**Angua**   I'm afraid it was Wolfgang who killed the semaphore agents . . .

**Carrot**   And Sleeps and Mr Skimmer.

**Angua**   Sir, I don't want there to be any trouble.

**Vimes**   He's been *killing* people! He's meddled with the dwarfs' affairs, he's stolen the Scone or swapped it or something! Cheery and Detritus are under arrest! Skimmer is dead! Sybil's locked up in your dad's castle! I've got to get back to Bonk. If they've harmed Sybil . . .

**Angua**   But he hasn't actually broken any rules in Überwald, sir. I'll talk to the wolves. See if they'll help.

*She crosses to* **Gavin** *and talks silently to him.*

**Vimes** (*to* **Carrot**)   Carrot? That wolf and Angua . . . ?

**Carrot**    They're old friends, sir.

**Vimes**    Right. Good. 'He's stolen the Scone' . . . No. No, he bloody hasn't. The bloody thing was never bloody stolen! Of course!

**Carrot**    Sir?

**Vimes**    All that stuff about swimming the lake and sleepy guards. That was all too risky. They needed a plan that would *work*. The Scone's not important, do you see? What's important is disarray – no king, violent arguments, fighting in the dark. And the king would be blamed because *he'd* lost the Scone. The bastards! I *knew* I nearly had it! It all fits if you don't think like a dwarf. Right, we're going to free Cheery and Detritus and then, Captain, we're going to . . .

**Carrot**    Prod buttock, sir?

**Vimes**    Right!

*Blackout.*


### Scene Six

*The von Überwald castle.* **Sybil** *and the* **Baroness** *are on-stage.*

**Sybil**    Are you *sure* there's been no more news?

**Baroness von Überwald**    Wolfgang and his friends are still out looking. But this is terrible weather for a man to be out on the run.

**Sybil**    He is *not* on the run! Sam is not guilty of anything!

**Baroness von Überwald**    Of course, of course. The evidence is purely circumstantial. I would suggest that, as soon as they have cleared the passes, you and your staff return to the safety of Ankh-Morpork before the real winter hits. We know the country, my dear, and if your husband is alive we can soon do something about it.

**Sybil**   I won't have him shamed like this. You *saw* him save the king!

**Baroness von Überwald**   I'm sure he did, Sybil. I fear I was talking to my husband at the time. Are you all right, my dear? You look a little tense.

**Sybil**   I do need to relax. Perhaps I could have a nice hot *bath*?

**Baroness von Überwald** (*reacting to the use of the 'b' word*) We do not, in fact, have a . . . such a device in the castle. We use the hot springs. So much more hygienic.

**Sybil**   Perhaps I'll have a lie down instead, then.

*She and the* **Baroness** *exit as the lights cross-fade to the exterior of the castle. Snow. Wind.* **Vimes** *enters, followed by* **Angua**, **Gavin**, **Carrot**, **Cheery**, **Detritus** *and* **Gaspode**.

**Vimes**   I know this is your family, Angua. I won't blame you if you hang back.

**Angua**   We'll see, sir, shall we?

**Carrot**   How are we going to get in, sir?

**Vimes**   How would *you* go about it, Carrot?

**Carrot**   Well, I'd start by knocking, sir.

**Vimes**   Really? Sergeant Detritus?

**Detritus**   Sir.

**Vimes**   Blow the bloody doors off.

**Detritus**   Yessir.

**Detritus** *aims his massive bow and fires. There is a huge explosion.*

**Vimes** (*to* **Carrot**)   This isn't Ankh-Morpork, see?

**Angua**   The wolves won't come in, sir. Gavin will follow me, but the rest of them aren't at home in houses.

**Vimes** (*drawing his sword*)   Right then – come on.

*They exit 'into' the castle. Lighting change.*

**Carrot**    Do you think they heard us, sir?

**Vimes**    Carrot, I should think *Ankh-Morpork* heard us. So – where are all the werewolves, then?

**Angua**    They'll be here. They'll leave us somewhere to run. We *always* leave people somewhere to run.

**Wolfgang**, *followed by some werewolves, enters.*

**Wolfgang**    Ah, Civilised! You won the game! Would you like another go? When people have a second game we give them a handicap! We bite one of their legs off! Good joke, hey?

**Vimes**    Where's my wife, you bastard?

**Wolfgang**    And Delphine! *Look* what the dog dragged in!

*He steps forward.* **Angua** *and* **Gavin** *growl. He stops and takes a step back.*

**Angua**    You haven't got the brains for this, Wolfie. And you couldn't plot your way out of a wet paper bag. Where's Mother? Hello Uncle Ulf, Aunt Hilda, Magwen (etc) – the pack's all here, then? What a family . . .

*The* **Baroness** *sweeps in.*

**Baroness von Überwald**    I want these disgusting people out of here *right* away! How dare you bring a troll into this house!

**Detritus** *raises his bow.*

How very *civilised.* How very Ankh-Morpork. You think you just have to threaten and the lesser races back down, eh? We're *werewolves.* Toys like that don't frighten us.

**Vimes**    Slow you down a bit though. Bring out Lady Sybil.

**Baroness von Überwald**    She's resting. You're in no position to make demands, Mister Vimes. We are not the criminal here. What is it you think we've done? Stolen the dwarfs' pet rock?

**Vimes**   You and I both *know* it wasn't stolen . . .

**Baroness von Überwald**   You *know* nothing! You suspect everything.

**Vimes**   Your son said . . .

**Baroness von Überwald**   My son unfortunately has no capacity for thought.

**Angua**   I can smell the fear, Mother. It's pouring off you.

**Sybil** *has entered. She carries an iron bar with a head-shaped bend in it.*

**Sybil**   Sam?

**Vimes**   Sybil! What's that . . . ?

**Sybil** (*looking at the iron bar*)   Oh. I got a bit fed up with being . . . guarded. *She* told me you were on the run and they were trying to save you. That wasn't right, was it?

**Vimes**   We've been having a lovely run in the woods, dear. Now please come here, because I think we're going to see the king. And I'm going to tell him everything. I've worked it out at last . . .

**Baroness von Überwald**   The dwarfs will *kill* you.

**Vimes**   I can probably out*run* a dwarf. And now we're leaving. Angua?

**Angua** *is still facing up to her mother.*

We are *leaving*, Angua.

**Carrot** *reaches and touches her arm. She turns sharply, snarling, but remembers herself instantly.*

**Baroness von Überwald**   So *this* is the boy? You betray your people for *this*? And what else has Ankh-Morpork taught you?

**Angua**   Self-control. Let's go, Mister Vimes. Don't turn your back. Don't run.

**Vimes**   Don't need telling. Detritus, don't fire unless you have to.

**Angua**   Don't worry, sir, they'd heal soon enough. Shoot anyway. Otherwise Wolfgang will pounce and the others will follow his lead . . .

**Carrot**   In that case, *I'll* deal with *him*.

**Carrot** *squares up, Victorian boxer-style, to* **Wolfgang**, *who advances, looking mildly amused.* **Wolfgang** *moves to grab one of* **Vimes**'s *party,* **Carrot** *intercepts him and lands a punch on him which seems to have no effect.* **Carrot** *goes to punch again but* **Wolfgang** *grabs his fist and holds it steady. He then squeezes, forcing* **Carrot** *to his knees (a knuckle-cracking SFX would be good).* **Angua** *steps forward.*

**Wolfgang** (*cheerfully*)   Do not try anything, Dephine Angua von überwald. Or else I will break his arm. Or perhaps I will break his arm anyway! Yes!

*There is a sickening crack.* **Carrot** *cries out in agony.*

And he has other bones! Get back, or I shall hurt him some more! No, I shall hurt him some more anyway!

*But* **Carrot** *has used his good arm to punch* **Wolfgang** *in the stomach.* **Wolfgang** *recovers immediately, punching* **Carrot** *so hard that he flies back across the stage.* **Wolfgang** *grabs* **Carrot** *and lifts him effortlessly to his feet.*

Civilised man! Here he is, sister!

*He 'throws' him to* **Angua**. *She kneels by him, distressed.*

Anyone else? How about you, civilised?

**Sybil**   Sam, you can't . . . !

**Vimes** *draws his sword. But* **Gavin** *suddenly galvanises into action, leaping at* **Wolfgang**, *pushing him momentarily off-stage,* *though* **Gavin** *remains on-stage. Strobe. When he re-appears,* **Wolfgang** *is in wolf form.*

**Gaspode**   That's no way to fight! He's gonna get *creamed*, fightin' like that! Stuff the rules, mate! *This* is how you win a dogfight, mate!

**Gavin** *and* **Gaspode** *both charge at '***Wolfgang***', forcing him back off-stage. There are animal cries and a huge splash.* **Detritus** *follows and returns immediately.*

**Detritus**   Dey've gone over der bridge into der moat, sir. Still fighting.

**Vimes**   Right. Go and find the von Überwald's Igor and bring him here. If anyone tries to stop you – shoot them. And shoot anyone standing near them.

**Detritus**   Sir.

**Vimes**   We're not a home to Mr Reasonable, Sergeant.

**Detritus**   I do not hear him knockin', sir.

**Detritus** *exits.*

**Vimes**   Go to it. Sergeant Angua?

**Angua**   How can you be so cool? He's *hurt*!

**Vimes**   I know. Cheery? Cover Carrot with something to keep him warm.

*He turns to the* **Baroness**.

And now, madam, you will give me the Scone of Stone.

**Baroness von Überwald**   Wolfgang will be back! That fall was *nothing!* And he'll *find* you!

**Vimes**   For the last time . . . the stone of the dwarfs. The wolves are waiting out there for you. The dwarfs are waiting in their city for *me*. Give me the stone and we might all survive. This is diplomacy. Don't let me try anything else.

**Baroness von Überwald**    I only have to say the word . . .

**Angua** *growls.* **Sybil** *strides forward and grabs the* **Baroness**.

**Sybil**    You never answered a single letter! All those years I wrote to you!

**Baroness von Überwald** (*to* **Vimes**)    If you know we have the Scone, then you know it's not the real one. And much good may it do the dwarfs!

**Vimes**    Yes, you had it made in Ankh-Morpork. But someone killed the man who did it, and that's against the law. That's something we have in Ankh-Morpork.

**Baroness von Überwald**    I know nothing about any deaths.

*Wolves howl, off.*

**Angua** *advances on the* **Baroness**.

**Angua**    Give him . . . the damn stone. Will any of you face me . . . *Now?* Then . . . give him the stone!

**Igor** *enters followed by* **Detritus**.

**Igor**    What theems to be the trouble?

*He sees* **Carrot** *and crosses to him.* **Angua** *continues to address the* **Baroness**.

**Angua**    Fetch the stone. And then . . . we . . . will leave. I can *smell* it. Or do you want me to *take it?*

*The* **Baroness** *runs off, the other werewolves back away into a corner.*

**Vimes** (*to* **Igor**)    If you can't help him then your future does not look good.

**Igor**    Narthty break on the arm. Wolfgang's work?

**Vimes**    Can you make him well?

**Igor**    It'th hith lucky day.

**Vimes**    We could use a man like you in the Watch, Igor.

**Igor**    Me, thir? Oh no, thir. But my nephew Igor ith looking for a pothition, marthter. And ith heart'th in the right plathe. I can thtate that for thertain, thir.

**Vimes**    Great. Let him know, would you?

**Igor**    Yeth, thir.

**Igor** *goes to tend to* **Carrot**.

**Vimes** (*to* **Angua**)    Look, Angua, I'm really sorry about, er, Gavin.

**Angua** (*flatly*)    Thanks. The moat runs straight to the Bonk Falls. No way he could have survived.

**Carrot**    He was a very noble creature. I am sorry he is dead. I'm sure we could have got on well. Gaspode went in the moat, too, sir. Brave little street fighter.

**Angua**    I'm going to check, though.

*She leaves as the* **Baroness** *enters, carrying the Scone.*

**Baroness von Überwald**    Take it. Take the wretched thing. It is a fake. No crime has been committed.

**Vimes**    I'm a policeman. I can always find a crime.

**Vimes** *takes the Scone from the* **Baroness** *as the lights black out.*


**Scene Seven**

*Meeting of the Überwald League of Temperance.* **Lady Margolotta** *in a spotlight. We hear her thoughts over the speakers.*

**Lady Margolotta's thoughts**    Here we go again. Actually, I quite like these meetings. They're a pretty mixed bunch but at least we share one conviction . . . what you were made isn't what you have to be or what you might become. The trick is to start small. Suck, but don't impale. Little steps. And then you find that all you really want is power and there are much politer ways of getting it than drinking people's blood. And then you realise that power is itself only a bauble – any thug can have power. The real prize is *control*. Lord Vetinari understands this. And all control starts with self.

**Lady Margolotta**    My name, in short form, is Lady Margolotta Amaya Katerina Assumpta Crassina von Überwald, and I am a vampire.

*Muted applause, off.*

It has been five years now. And I am still taking one night at a time. One neck will always be too many. But . . . there are compensations . . .

*Lights black out.*

## Scene Eight

*The dwarf kingdom. A couple of dwarf guards, on.* **Vimes**, **Cheery**, **Sybil**, **Carrot** *and* **Detritus** *enter.* **Vimes** *has the Scone in a large sack.*

**Dwarf Guard**    You? You are under arrest!

**Vimes**    You will have heard that the Scone was stolen?

**Dwarf Guard**    What of it?

**Vimes**    Look!

*He opens the sack and the guards look in. They fall to their knees.*

I want to take this to the king.

*The guards mutter together.* **Vimes** *turns to* **Cheery**.

What's going on?

**Cheery Littlebottom**    There's no precedent for this. You're supposed to be an assassin, but you've come back to see the king and you have the Scone . . .

**Vimes**   Right. Where's Angua, by the way?

**Cheery Littlebottom**   She and the wolves are searching the river for . . . well for bodies, sir. Gavin, sir.

**Vimes**   Yes, and that bloody Wolfgang.

**Dee** *bursts on.*

**Dee**   They are to be arrested! He attempted to kill the king! He escaped from his cell!

**Vimes**   That's something about which we might hear more evidence. You can't always keep people in the dark, Dee.

**Dee**   You will not see the king!

**Vimes** (*taking out the Scone and holding it aloft*)   Then I shall smash the Scone!

**Dee**   Do so! It won't . . .

**Vimes** (*quietly*)   It won't *what*? It won't matter? But this is the *Scone*!

**Dee**   I . . . that is . . . the king . . . you may give it to *me*.

**Sybil** (*snapping*)   Absolutely not! When Ironhammer returned the Scone to Bloodaxe in your legends, would he have given it to Slogram?

*The dwarfs on-stage murmur dissent.*

**Dee**   Of course not! But he was a trait –

**Vimes** (*calmly*)   I think . . . that we had better see the king, don't you?

**Rhys Rhysson** *enters with* **Albrecht**.

**Rhys Rhysson**   Ah, your excellency. I see you have something that belongs to us?

**Dee**   That thing. That thing is . . . a fake, sire. A copy. Made in Ankh-Morpork! Part of a plot which, I am sure can be proven, involves milord Vimes! It is *not* the Scone!

**Rhys Rhysson** (*looking at the Scone*)   I have seen the Scone many times before. And I would say this appears to be the true thing and the whole of the thing.

**Dee**   Sire, I demand . . . er, that is, I advise you to demand a closer inspection, sire.

**Rhys Rhysson**   Really? Well, I am not an expert, see? But we are fortunate, are we not, that Albrecht Albrechtson is here for the coronation. He is the authority on the Scone and its history. Albrecht. Your opinion, please, on the veracity of this Scone.

**Albrecht** *examines the Scone closely. He takes out his knife, chips a piece off and eats it. After a while, he declares:*

**Albrecht Albrechtson**   Pak-gah. Ah Pak-gah ad Huh-gradz.

*The crowd reacts.*

**Cheery Littlebottom** (*to* **Vimes**)   'It is the true thing, and the whole of the thing . . .'

**Vimes** (*aside, to* **Cheery**)   Blimey! When we make a forgery in Ankh-Morpork, it's better than the real damn thing! . . . Unless. Unless I'm missing something . . . ?

**Rhys Rhysson**   Thank you, Albrecht. If everyone could leave us, please. Except Dee, milord Vimes and milady Sybil . . . ?

*All file out.*

And now, Dee, go and fetch my axe, would you?

**Dee**   But, sire! This man's ancestor killed a king!

**Rhys Rhysson**   I imagine they've got it out of their system, then. Now, do as I say.

**Dee** *exits.*

Now, your blackboard monitorship. Tell me everything. Tell me the *truth*.

**Vimes**    I'm not sure I know it any more.

**Rhys Rhysson**    A good start. Tell me what you suspect, then.

**Vimes**    Sire, I'd swear that thing is as fake as a tin shilling.

**Rhys Rhysson**    Really?

**Vimes**    The *real* Scone wasn't stolen, it was destroyed. I reckon it was smashed up and mixed in with the sand in its cave. You see, sire, if people see something's gone, and then you turn up with something that looks like it, they'll think, 'This must be it, because it isn't where we thought it was.' I'm sorry, I haven't had much sleep . . .

**Rhys Rhysson**    You're doing very well for a sleep-walking man.

**Vimes**    The thief was working with the werewolves, I think. They were going to blackmail you off the throne. Well, you *know* that. To keep Überwald in the dark. If you *didn't* step down, there'd be a war, and if you *did* Albrecht would get the fake Scone.

**Rhys Rhysson**    And what else do you think you know?

**Vimes**    Well, the fake was made in Ankh-Morpork. I *think* someone had the maker killed, but I can't find out more 'til I get back.

**Rhys Rhysson**    To fool Albrecht, you must have made it very well.

**Vimes**    Is it possible Albrecht was involved?

**Rhys Rhysson**    No. Who was it said: 'Where you find crimes, you find policemen?'

**Vimes**    Er, me.

**Rhys Rhysson**    I imagine Dee should have had time to think by now . . . Ah.

**Dee** *enters, carrying* **Rhys**'s *axe. He offers it to* **Rhys**, *who indicates for him to place it on the floor.*

Place your hands on the Scone, Dee.

**Dee**   Sire?

**Rhys Rhysson**   Do as I say. Now.

**Dee** *does so.*

Tell me about the death of the candle captain.

**Dee** (*turning to him*)   Oh, as I told you, sire . . .

**Rhys Rhysson**   If you do not keep your hands pressed on the stone, Dee, I will see to it that they are fixed there. Tell me *again*.

**Dee**   I . . . he . . . took his own life, sire. Out of shame.

**Rhys Rhysson** (*picking up the axe. To* **Vimes**)   There's an old tradition, see, that since the Scone contains a grain of Truth, it will glow red hot if a lie is told by anyone touching it. Of course, in these modern times, I shouldn't think anyone believes it. (*Speaking calmly.*) Tell me again.

**Dee** (*getting more stressed*)   He took his own life, sire!

**Rhys Rhysson**   Oh yes. You said. And do you recall, Dee, when Slogram sent false word of Bloodaxe's death to Ironhammer, causing Ironhammer to take his own life in grief, where was the guilt?

**Dee** (*automatically*)   It was Slogram's, sire.

**Rhys Rhysson**   Yes. And who gave the order to kill the craftsman in Ankh-Morpork?

**Dee**   Sire?

**Rhys Rhysson** (*in the same tone as the first time he asked*)   Who gave the order to kill the craftsman in Ankh-Morpork?

**Dee**   I know nothing about . . .

**Rhys Rhysson**   Guards, press his hands firmly against the Scone.

*The guards do so.*

Who gave the order?

**Dee** (*who clearly now believes his hands are getting hotter*)   I . . . I . . .

**Rhys Rhysson**   *Who?*

**Dee**   Not me! I said they must take all necessary steps to preserve secrecy!

**Rhys Rhysson**   To whom did you say this?

**Dee**   I can give you names!

**Rhys Rhysson**   Later, you will. I can promise you that, boyo. And the werewolves?

**Dee**   The baroness suggested it!

**Rhys Rhysson**   Überwald for the werewolves. Ah yes. 'Joy Through Strength'. I expect they promised you all sorts of things. But – my predecessors always spoke very highly of you. Why did you do it? Why let yourself become a paw of the werewolves?

**Dee** (*snapping*)   Why should they be allowed to get away with it?

**Rhys Rhysson**   Oh, I suspect that the werewolves will not . . .

**Dee**   Not *them*! The . . . ones in Ankh-Morpork! Wearing . . . make-up and dresses and . . . and abominable things!

**Dee** *points at* **Cheery**. *He breaks down into tears during the following.*

Hah-*ack*! How can you even *look* at it? You let *her* flaunt herself here! It's happening because people have not been firm, not obeyed, let the old ways slide! How can you be king and allow this? You do nothing! Everywhere they are doing it and you do nothing! Why should *they* be allowed to do this? *I* can't!

**Rhys Rhysson**   I see. Well, I suppose that is *an* explanation. (*To the guards.*) Take . . . *her* away.

**Cheery Littlebottom**   Permission to go with her, sire?

**Rhys Rhysson**   What on earth for, young w . . . young dwarf?

**Cheery Littlebottom**   I expect she'd like someone to talk to, sire. I know I would.

**Rhys Rhysson** (*looking at* **Vimes**, *who nods*)   Very well.

**Cheery**, **Dee** *and the guards leave.*

Well, your excellency?

**Vimes**   But he . . . she believed in the Scone! But it *is* a fake. Isn't it?

**Rhys Rhysson**   You are not certain?

**Vimes**   Dee was!

**Rhys Rhysson**   Dee is in a difficult state of mind. But, yes, this is the real Scone.

**Vimes**   But how could . . . ?

**Rhys Rhysson**   Wait. So was the one that was ground to dust in its cave by Dee in, her, madness. So were the, let me see, five before that. What – still untouched by time after fifteen hundred years? What romantics dwarfs are! Even the very best dwarf bread crumbles after a few hundred.

**Vimes**   Fakes? They were all fakes?

**Rhys Rhysson** (*holding up his axe*)   Milord, this is my family's axe. We have owned it for almost nine hundred years, see. Of course, sometimes it has needed a new blade. Sometimes a new handle, new designs on the metalwork and so on. But it is still my family's axe, handed down over generations.

**Vimes**　Hold on. Albrecht *knew*.

**Rhys Rhysson**　Oh yes. A number of the senior dwarfs know. The knowledge runs in families. The first Scone crumbled after three hundred years. After that, we were more prepared. We'd have needed a new one in a few years anyway and I'm happy it was made in the large dwarf city of Ankh-Morpork.

**Vimes**　But Albrecht could have exposed you.

**Rhys Rhysson**　Exposed *what*? He is not king, but one of his family will be in the fullness of time. What goes around, comes around, as the Igors say. You think because Albrecht has old-fashioned ideas he is a bad dwarf. That is not the case. I have known him for two hundred years and he is an honorable man. We are all floating in the same boat. We may try to push one another over the side but only a maniac like Dee would make a hole in the bottom. You're tired. Let your lady take you home for a well-earned rest.

**Vimes**　Ankh-Morpork wants the names of the murderers.

**Rhys Rhysson**　No, that is what *Commander Vimes* wants. What does Ankh-Morpork want? Gold. Or iron. You use a lot of iron.

**Vimes** (*weakly*)　Fat. Lots of fat.

**Rhys Rhysson**　Well, certainly. That too. The price is ten cents a barrel but, your excellency, since I have come to know you, I feel that perhaps . . .

**Sybil** (*interrupting*)　Five cents a barrel for Grade One rendered, three cents for Grade Two, ten cents a barrel for heavy tallow, safe and delivered to Ankh-Morpork. All taken from the Schmalzberg Levels – I'm not too happy with the quality of the Big Tusk Wells.

*She sees that* **Vimes** *is looking at her incredulously.*

I did a bit of reading while you were out, dear. Sorry.

**Rhys Rhysson**　Would you beggar us, madam?

**Sybil**   We may be flexible on delivery.

**Rhys Rhysson**   Klatch would pay at least nine cents for Grade One.

**Sybil**   But the Klatchian Ambassador isn't here.

**Rhys Rhysson** (*smiling*)   Or married to you, my lady, much to his loss. Very well. Price to remain stable for two years. The paperwork will be with you in the morning.

**Cheery** *re-enters.*

Ah, Miss Littlebottom. May I say how much I admire your . . . sartorial courage. (*Speaking slightly sotto voce.*) You must let me know the name of your dressmaker. I may have some custom for her in the fullness of time.

**Cheery Littlebottom** (*with a gulp*)   Yes, your majesty.

**Rhys** *shakes* **Cheery**'s *hand. The dwarfs all leave.* **Cheery** *turns to* **Lady Sybil**.

Did you hear what the king said . . . ? That was as good as saying that *he* is a . . .

**Sybil**   Things are going to change. That's what the king was saying. Right, Sam, let's get you back to the embassy. Time we went home, I think.

*Blackout.*


## Scene Nine

*Back at the embassy.* **Igor** *is just ushering in* **Vimes** *and* **Sybil**.

**Igor**   Welcome back, marthter and mithtreth.

**Vimes**   Thank you, Igor.

**Igor** *exits.*

So that's it, is it? Bloody politics again? Dee'll get off with a few days breaking rocks, or bread, or whatever they do. After all, she only smashed a fake.

**Sybil**   But she *thought* she was committing a much bigger crime, Sam.

**Vimes**   Yeah. And that ought to count for something. Bloody baroness is guilty as hell, too. People *died*. As for Wolfgang . . .

**Sybil**   Surely even he couldn't have survived that waterfall.

**Vimes**   I dunno, but I just don't believe he's dead. Any sensible person would flee the country, but we're talking about *Wolfgang*. A dog returns to his vomit, a fool returns to his folly. Well, that's Wolfgang on both counts. He's going to be back. I can feel it in my water.

**Sybil**   Sam, Wolfgang is Angua's problem, not yours. Sam, I need to talk to you. Sam, I'm going to have a baby.

**Vimes**   I just know he's going . . . What? How?

**Sybil**   The normal way, I hope. Mrs Content is quite sure, and she's been a midwife for fifty years.

**Vimes** (*stunned*)   Oh. Good. That's good.

**Sybil**   It'll probably take a while to sink in.

**Vimes**   Right. Everything will be all right, will it? I mean, you're rather . . . er, um . . . you're not as . . .

**Sybil**   Sam, my family have *bred* for breeding. Of course everything will be all right.

**Vimes**   Oh. Good.

*There is a crash, off, followed by a wolf howl and a scream, cut off short.*

It's Wolfgang! Quick! Go and lock yourself in the dining room!

**Sybil**    But . . .

**Vimes**    Just *do it*!! But don't strain yourself.

**Sybil** *exits, hurriedly.* **Igor** *staggers on, helped by* **Cheery** *and* **Detritus**. *He collapses.*

Can you do anything for him, Cheery?

**Cheery** *shakes her head.*

**Igor**    Marthter, you got to remember thith, right?

**Vimes**    What?

**Igor**    You got to get me to the ithehouthe downthtairth and let Igor know, underthtand?

**Vimes**    Which Igor?

**Igor**    Any Igor! My heartth had it, but my liverth ath right ath ninepenthe, tell him! Remember, what goeth around, cometh around.

*He dies.*

**Cheery Littlebottom**    He's gone, sir.

**Vimes**    Right. I've got to find Wolfgang. You two get Igor to the icehouse and then get back here.

**Cheery** *and* **Detritus** *drag* **Igor** *out.* **Wolfgang** *appears.*

**Wolfgang**    Hello, Civilised! You wait for me, hey?

**Wolfgang** *starts to advance on* **Vimes**. *Strobe on.* **Angua** *(wolf) bursts on and barges* **Wolfgang** *into the wings. They emerge immediately, with* **Wolfgang** *also in wolf form and fight.* **Detritus** *appears on the balcony with his bow.*

**Vimes** (*to* **Detritus**)    No! You'll hit Angua too!

**Detritus**    Not a problem, sir. It won't kill them, but it'll slow Wolfgang down a bit.

**Angua** *has thrown* **Wolfgang** *into the wings again, and he emerges as a man again.*

**Vimes** (*to* **Angua**)   Go to it, Angua! He doesn't know whether to fight you as a wolf or as a man! You've got him confused! Make the most of it!

**Wolfgang** *now grabs* **Angua** *(wolf) and hurls her off-stage. He bounds out of the room. A pause and* **Angua** *(human) re-enters.*

**Vimes** (*crossing to her*)   It's all right, he's gone.

**Angua**   It's *not* all right! He'll lie low and then he'll be back! I *know* him! He'll track us down and then he'll kill Carrot!

**Vimes**   Carrot? Why?

**Angua**   Because he's *mine*.

**Cheery** *and* **Detritus** *enter.*

**Vimes**   You two, help Angua. I think I want to make an arrest. Wolfgang has murdered someone on Ankh-Morpork soil. Here in the Embassy. That makes him *mine*.

*They help* **Angua** *out.*

Now then what kills werewolves? Silver, of course, and fire. Fire? Hold on . . .

*He rummages in his bag and produces the grenade he pocketed at the semaphore tower.*

Fire. Right then, little doggy, let's be having . . .

**Wolfgang** *appears suddenly. He is in human form, but has a wolf ear and arm and seems confused and edgy.*

**Wolfgang**   Mister Civilised? You want another game?

**Vimes**   Still not sure if you're wolf or man, eh? That must be very confusing for you. You're guilty of murder on Ankh-Morpork territory. I am an officer of the law, I am armed . . .

**Wolfgang**   Armed? With a distress flare grenade?

**Vimes**   . . . And you are under arrest.

**Wolfgang**   Ah, this is 'civilised', is it?

**Vimes**    Yes, this is how we do it. You understand what I'm saying to you? You're under arrest, so come along quietly.

**Wolfgang**    Hah! Your Ankh-Morpork sense of humour.

**Vimes**    Yes, I'll drop my trousers next. You're not resisting arrest, are you? *Are you?*

**Wolfgang**    Of course I am you silly man! Good joke, this!

**Vimes**    Perhaps we might appeal to your doggy side then?

**Wolfgang**    What do you mean?

**Vimes**    We-e-ll, I already know you don't like words like *vet* (**Wolfgang** *winces.*) or *bath.* (**Wolfgang** *winces again.*) Funny that, isn't it? *Vet.* (*Reaction.*) *Bath.* (*Reaction.*)

*He takes out the grenade and lights it.*

I *am* armed. Don't force me to use this.

**Wolfgang**    A distress flare? You bore me, civilised. I think I had better kill you.

**Vimes**    Let's try another doggie word, then . . .

**Vimes** *tosses the grenade at* **Wolfgang**. *Either* **Wolfgang** *catches it and steps back into the wings with it, or it falls into the wings . . .* **Wolfgang** *hesitates, for a moment, then bounds off after the grenade. There is an explosion, off, and* **Wolfgang**'s *arm flies on and lands in front of* **Vimes**. *It is important that* **Vimes** *does not speak until* **Wolfgang** *is dead.*

Fetch.

*Blackout.*


**Scene Ten**

*Exterior. Snow on ground. Bells tolling.* **Vimes** *enters.* **Lady Margolotta** *enters simultaneously, from a different entrance. She is now in more traditional vampire gear.*

**Lady Margolotta**   Your excellency? We didn't get a chance to speak at the coronation. I heard about Wolfgang. Well done.

**Vimes**   I told him. I warned him. I told him he was under arrest.

**Lady Margolotta**   I wouldn't doubt it, Commander.

**Vimes**   Told him I was armed, too. But he resisted arrest.

**Lady Margolotta**   Yes. I know. You followed the rules, Commander. Clearly you were not to know he would automatically catch the explosive. The dog-like qualities of the werewolf could hardly have occurred to a man from the big city.

**Vimes**   That's right. Laws are meant to be there to be used. So – now he's gone and that's one up for the vampires, eh?

**Lady Margolotta**   I would like to think that it's a blessing for the whole country. Wolfgang was a throwback – a sadistic murderer who frightened even his own family. Delphine . . . Angua . . . will have some peace of mind. The world will be a better place.

**Vimes**   I just don't see how he could've come back after that fall into the river . . . wait – you *helped* him to come back. Just like you helped me.

**Lady Margolotta**   He'd have come back anyway, sooner or later. Some time when you weren't expecting him. And he'd have tracked Angua like a wolverine. Best that things ended today. So yes, I *did* help.

**Vimes**   But you just left me in the snow. You couldn't have known I'd beat him.

**Lady Margolotta**   Havelock Vetinari wouldn't have sent a fool to Überwald. At least, not a *stupid* fool.

**Vimes**   You've *met* him, haven't you?

**Lady Margolotta**   Lord Vetinari? Yes.

**Vimes**   But how – no, hang on . . . why are you *here*. Now? And dressed like that . . . ?

**Lady Margolotta**   For Igor's funeral, of course.

**Vimes**   But he's only just . . .

*A row of* **Igors** *enter and cross the stage. Each carries a metal box with frosting on the outside. One carries the dead* **Igor***'s tailcoat and boots.*

What? A funeral – with party loot bags? Everyone gets something to take home?

**Igor** (*whoever!!*)   You could thay that, thir. But we think that putting bodieth into the ground ith rather gruethome. All thothe wormth and thingth. Thith way, he'll mothtly be up and about in no time.

**Vimes**   Reincarnation on the installment plan, eh?

**Igor**   Motht amuthing, thir. Thethe will all be put to good uthe, thir. By tonight, there will be thome lucky people in thethe partth.

**Vimes**   And these parts in some lucky people?

**Igor**   Well done, thir. I can thee you are a wit. And thome day thome poor thoul will have a narthty brain injury. (*He taps the box he is carrying.*) And . . .

**Vimes** *joins in and says this with him.*

What goeth around cometh around.
Well, I mutht be going now, thir. Tho much to do. You know how it ith.

*He exits.*

**Lady Margolotta**   It's been good to have met you, excellency. I'm sure we shall meet again. Do give my fondest regards to Havelock.

**Vimes**   Er . . . right. Well, I'd better get Sybil.

**Lady Margolotta**    Have a safe journey.

*They shake hands and exit their separate ways.*

**Carrot** *and* **Angua** *enter.* **Carrot** *is carrying a shovel.*

**Angua**    That was good of you.

**Carrot**    It had to be done. Gavin was a brave wolf and deserved a proper burial. No sign of Gaspode, though.

**Angua**    Gaspode's a street fighter. He'll be back.

**Carrot**    I noticed there were lots of wolf tracks around.

**Angua**    They won't have stayed. Wolves look to the future. They don't try to remember things.

**Carrot**    They're lucky.

**Angua**    They're just realistic. The future contains their next meal and their next danger. Is your arm all right?

**Carrot**    It feels as good as new. Recruiting an Igor to the Watch was very clever of Mister Vimes.

**Angua**    Carrot! Don't *you* remember last night? Didn't you wonder what *I* might become? Don't you worry about the future? Wolfgang was my brother – it could be a family trait . . . all werewolves have to struggle with being two things at once and never quite being either of them fully. We're not the most stable of creatures.

**Carrot**    Gold and muck come out of the same shaft.

**Angua**    That's just a dwarf saying.

**Carrot**    It's true, though. But you're not Wolfgang.

**Angua**    Well, if it happened. If it *did*. Would you do what Vimes did? Would it be you who came after me? Would it be *you*?

**Carrot**    Yes.

**Angua**    Promise?

**Carrot** *takes her hand as* **Vimes** *and* **Sybil** *enter.*

**Vimes**    Well, it was a very . . . interesting coronation.

**Sybil**    You were bored out of your skull.

**Vimes**    Yes, well, it *was* dull. I was expecting a bit more . . .

**Sybil**    It's a very old ceremony, Sam. Dull, perhaps, but dullness distilled and cultivated over the years into quite an impressive show.

**Vimes**    And the Scone didn't explode, or crumble, or glow red-hot. I 'spose it really *is* the real one, now. (*Pause.*) Here, how come Cheery didn't wear a frock, then. To the coronation, like? Just ordinary dwarf clothes.

**Sybil**    Because she could have if she'd wanted, Sam, that's why. *Now* she's free to wear what she likes and she doesn't have to wear a dress if she doesn't want to.

**Carrot**    A bit of snow overnight, sir, but the road looks open. They say there's a big storm due tonight, though, so we should . . .

**Vimes**    You fit enough to travel?

**Angua**    We both are.

**Vimes**    You two and the others can go on ahead. Sybil and I will take the other coach. Or possibly a sleigh. We'll just . . . take it a bit easier. See the sights. We'll dawdle along the way. Understand?

**Carrot**    Yes, sir.

**Angua** *and* **Sybil** *exchange knowing nods.*

**Vimes**    Oh, and there's three gloomy biddies living in a big house nearby. It's got a cherry orchard. Find out the address and when you get back send them three coach tickets to Ankh-Morpork.

**Carrot**    Right, sir.

**Vimes**   Well done. Travel safely. I'll see you in a week. Or two. Three at the outside. All right?

**Carrot**   Sir.

**Carrot** *and* **Angua** *leave.*

**Vimes**   After all, we can't have you rattling around in some fast coach in your condition, can we?

**Sybil**   And *you* need a break. I know you feel guilty about it, but they'll cope. It's time you took a week out.

**Vimes**   Or two.

**Sybil/Vimes**   Three at the outside.

*They saunter off. Blackout.*